TRENCHERMAN'S

Guide

partners

THE
eco
LAUNDRY
that doesn't cost the earth

90th
HALLGARTEN
& NOVUM WINES
1933-2023

NAVAS
PREMIUM BOTANICAL MIXERS

PKF
FRANCIS
CLARK
Shared Ambition

TREVETHAN
Cornish Craft Distillery

EDITOR
Abi Manning

EDITORIAL TEAM
Ting Baker
Kathryn Lewis
Melissa Morris
Kirstie Newton
Rosanna Rothery
Melissa Stewart
Selena Young

EDITORIAL DIRECTOR
Jo Rees

DESIGN
Christopher Mulholland
Dale Stiling

COMMERCIAL
Claire Fegan
Jeni Smith

PUBLISHING
Charlotte Cummins
Tamsin Powell

MANAGING DIRECTOR
Nick Cooper

PUBLISHED BY SALT MEDIA
ideas@saltmedia.co.uk
01271 859299
saltmedia.co.uk

FSC
www.fsc.org

MIX
Paper from
responsible sources
FSC® C019670

Foreword

If you're holding this new edition of the *Trencherman's Guide*, the likelihood is you appreciate authenticity, creativity and innovation – the exact qualities championed within its pages.

For over 31 years the guide has celebrated the food-rich region of the South West, its produce and its people. Because at the heart of every Trencherman's member restaurant are its people: pastry chefs pouring their all into perfecting desserts, chefs braving blustery coastlines to forage samphire for tomorrow's menu, sommeliers sniffing out the perfect South West white to pair with chef's monkfish, and front of house managers delivering the warm-yet-polished service that elevates a dining experience. It's this passion that gives each venue the unique character and charm that's so often lacking in chain restaurants.

hospitality sector and the artisan food and drink producers that supply the kitchens.

As the new editor of the guide, I raise a glass to everyone working behind the scenes at the 106 restaurants listed in this 31st edition; they are the reason this region is such a gastronomic hotspot.

Consider the guide your passport to a year of incredible feasting.

'At the heart of every member restaurant are its people'

I encourage you to seek out these authentic dining experiences in the knowledge that you are supporting ingenuity and talent in the

Abi Manning
Editor

Contents

The Barrington Boar | p140

Welcome to the 31st edition of the *Trencherman's Guide.*

Each edition of the guide has its own unique personality, a result of the varied mix of restaurants contained within its pages. This year is no different and it's fascinating to see how the industry has developed during the past 12 months.

I'm especially impressed by the line-up of young and upcoming chefs and chef-owners. It's so encouraging to witness talented young people who've been nurtured in the South West having the drive to launch their own restaurants in the region. You only need look at the winners and finalists of this year's Trencherman's Awards to see some of these ambitious men and women.

'It's so encouraging to witness talented young people having the drive to launch their own restaurants'

Another interesting development has been the way in which chefs and restaurateurs have extended their core business to incorporate a variety of dining experiences – from wood-fired pizzas in hotel gardens to laid-back, family-friendly venues that don't compromise on quality. It's opening up authentic, independent South West dining experiences to an even greater audience, which is fantastic for everyone, including the South West's food and drink producers.

Enjoy the guide.

Michael Caines MBE
Chairman of the Trencherman's committee

TRENCHERMAN'S

AWARDS
2023

Following 30,000 votes from readers, the winners of the Trencherman's Awards 2023 were crowned in March at a spectacular ceremony at Salcombe Harbour Hotel in Devon.

Meet the winners and finalists of the prestigious awards and get a sneak peek at what went down during the evening.

Photographs by Guy Harrop

Trencherman's readers and food lovers across the South West came out in force to support their favourite restaurants, hotels, pubs, chefs and front-of-house teams in the Trencherman's Awards 2023. Over 30,000 individual votes were cast, and we had some of the closest final scores in the awards' ten-year history.

The winners were crowned at a sparkling Trencherman's Awards ceremony and dinner by the sea at Salcombe Harbour Hotel in Devon. It was hosted by broadcaster and food critic William Sitwell, chef and restaurateur Mark Hix of The Oyster & Fish House and Trencherman's editorial director Jo Rees.

William Sitwell said: *'Very few areas of the country have a guide like Trencherman's, which rivals Hardens or Michelin in terms of how it's put together. The* Trencherman's Guide *has experienced and knowledgeable food writers bringing their know-how and knowledge to it, and the South West food scene has the most extraordinary talent.*

'The Trencherman's Awards showcase incredible talent, innovation, a lot of energy, and the many young people who have come into the hospitality business – and of course a few true stalwarts like my co-host Mark Hix.'

The finale of the evening saw Nathan Outlaw win the Award for Special Contribution. Nathan said: *'To receive this award is incredible and a great honour.*

'I've been in the South West for well over 25 years and the Trencherman's Guide *has always been at the forefront of the scene. It's one of the guides you want to get into as a chef.*

'I don't think there are many guides in the UK, let alone the world, that have got 30 years under their belt, and it shows how amazing the South West is – from the hotels to the guesthouses, bars and restaurants – and it's only getting better and better.'

'It's one of the guides you want to get into as a chef'

In traditional Trencherman's style, a number of last year's award winners made up the team of top chefs who crafted the ceremony's four-course feast: Mark Dodson of The Masons Arms (starter), Michael Smith of Porthminster Beach Café (fish course), Jamie Gulliford of Salcombe Harbour Hotel (main) and Dorian Janmaat of The Idle Rocks (dessert).

The chefs crafted dishes using fabulously fresh produce provided by Dole, Matthew Stevens Cornish Fish and Gibbins Quality Meats, while each course was paired with the finest wines from Hallgarten & Novum Wines, top-notch beers from Sharp's Brewery and soft drinks from Frobishers. Canapés were served with local spirits: Trevethan Cornish Gin, Atlantic Spirit No.7 Sea Buckthorn Gin and Sea Arch Coastal Juniper.

Winners and finalists

Award for Special Contribution
Sponsored by PKF Francis Clark

Winner
Nathan Outlaw – Outlaw's

Grand finalists
Paul Ainsworth – Paul Ainsworth at No6
Kit Chapman – The Castle at Taunton
Geetie Singh-Watson – The Bull Inn

Best Trencherman's Chef
Sponsored by Hallgarten & Novum Wines

Winner
Andrew Swann – The Castle at Taunton

Grand finalists
Harriet Mansell – Robin Wylde
James Harris – The Beckford Bottle Shop
Joshua Jones – Number Eight

Best Trencherman's Restaurant

Sponsored by Dole

Winner
Prawn on the Lawn, Padstow

Grand finalists
Robin Wylde, Lyme Regis
Ronnie's of Thornbury, near Bristol
The Angel – Taste of Devon, Dartmouth

Best Trencherman's Hotel

Sponsored by The Eco Laundry

Winner
Boringdon Hall Hotel, Plymouth

Grand finalists
Lewtrenchard Manor, Okehampton
Talland Bay Hotel, Porthallow
The Castle at Taunton

Best Trencherman's Pub

Winner

The Castle Inn, Castle Combe

Grand finalists

The Barrington Boar, Ilminster

The Cotley Inn, Wambrook

The Lord Poulett Arms, Hinton St George

Best Front of House Team

Winner

Crab House Cafe, Wyke Regis

Grand finalists

Hooked on the Rocks, Falmouth

Millside, Lyme Regis

The Dartmoor Inn, Lydford

Best Bar List

Winner

The Farmers Arms, Woolsery

Grand finalists

New Coast Kitchen, Croyde

Robun, Bath

The Idle Rocks, St Mawes

Award for Creativity & Innovation

Sponsored by Sharp's Brewery

Winner

Ugly Butterfly by Adam Handling, Carbis Bay

Grand finalists

Appleton's Bar & Restaurant, Fowey

Brassica Restaurant, Beaminster

The Angel – Taste of Devon, Dartmouth

Best Newcomer

Sponsored by Salt Media

Winner

Andria, Dartmouth

Grand finalists

New Coast Kitchen, Croyde

The Rocket Store, Boscastle

Thornbury Castle, near Bristol

Trencherman's Awards 2023 winners are also highlighted throughout the guide.

More ways to discover exquisite dining in the South West

Second helpings

Get a second helping of the *Trencherman's Guide* by signing up to the regular email newsletter. It shares the low-down on events and openings across the region, features interviews with chefs and reveals great places to eat out.

You'll also receive advance notification of voting for the annual Trencherman's Awards.

Sign up to the newsletter at
trenchermans-guide.com/ join-the-club

Digital Trencherman's

Want to browse more images of the restaurants in the guide? Or left your copy of the *Trencherman's Guide* at home and need a dining recommendation on the hoof? The Trencherman's website ensures you're only ever a few clicks away from finding the best places to eat out in the South West.

trenchermans-guide.com

Be social

Stay up to date with the latest foodie news via the Trencherman's social channels.

f   The Trenchermans Guide

X   @trenchermans

◎   @trenchermans_guide

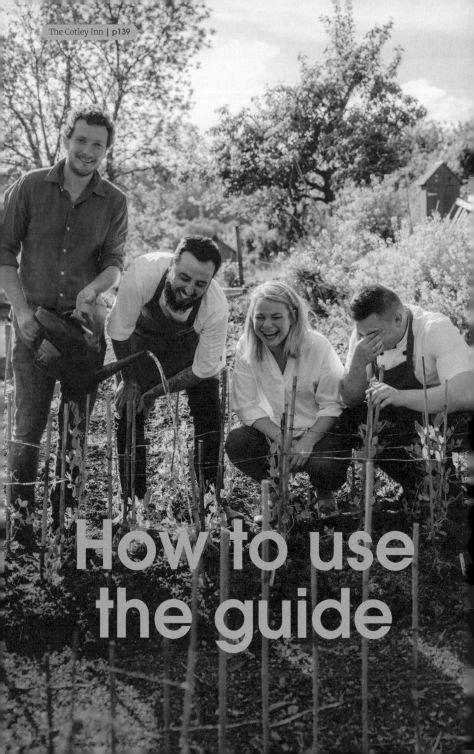

How to use the guide

Restaurants are only invited into the guide after surpassing strict scoring criteria, so you can be confident they deliver a seriously good dining experience.

To make the guide easy to use, the restaurants are grouped into geographical regions. You will find each venue plotted on a map at the beginning of each section, with a map number that's mirrored on each profile page. Alternatively, flick to a chosen restaurant by finding its page number in the index in the back.

Look for these symbols throughout the guide

 Restaurants that have achieved an exceptionally high Trencherman's score and been identified as a Higher Member

 Restaurants where you can stay the night

This year we have also added details about EV charging facilities at the restaurants.

Cornwall

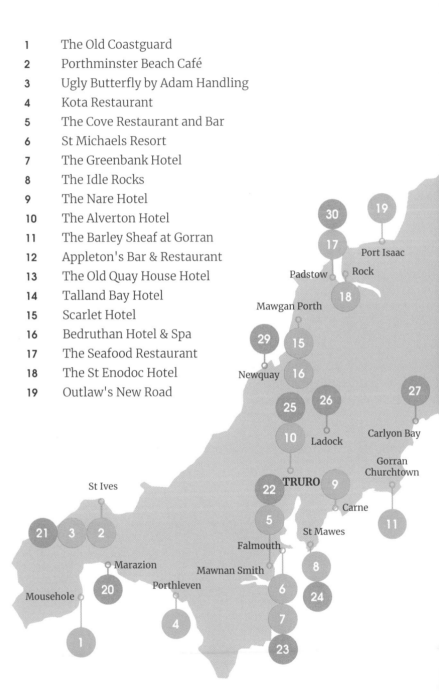

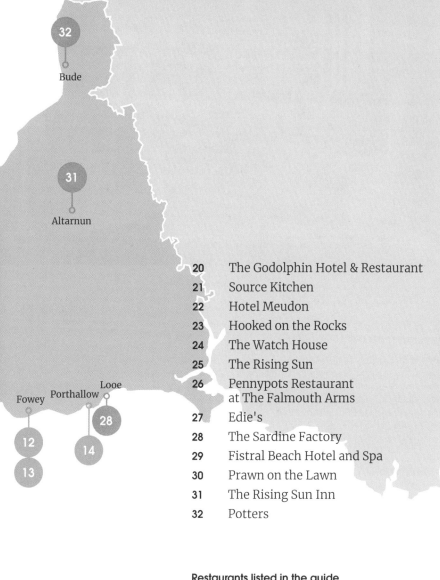

20 The Godolphin Hotel & Restaurant

21 Source Kitchen

22 Hotel Meudon

23 Hooked on the Rocks

24 The Watch House

25 The Rising Sun

26 Pennypots Restaurant
   at The Falmouth Arms

27 Edie's

28 The Sardine Factory

29 Fistral Beach Hotel and Spa

30 Prawn on the Lawn

31 The Rising Sun Inn

32 Potters

**Restaurants listed in the guide
correspond to the numbers
plotted on the map.**

All locations are approximate

1 The Old Coastguard

Delicious simplicity

Part of Charles and Edmund Inkin's Eatdrinksleep stable (sister venues include chef fave The Gurnard's Head near Zennor and The Felin Fach Griffin in Brecon), The Old Coastguard is a restaurant with rooms in the beautiful fishing village of Mousehole.

Its menu is dictated by what's local and in season. Newlyn's dayboats tie up a mere two miles west so fish is a given, but head chef Danny Garland also pays homage to the superb meats, cheeses and vegetables on the restaurant's doorstep.

There are three charming places to dine: at scrubbed wooden tables on the Upper Deck with views to St Clement's Isle, on the Sun Deck with just a pane of glass separating diners from the palm trees or, best of all, on the terrace looking down at the sun-dappled sea.

The menu may be rooted in traditional brasserie-style cooking, but when ingredients this good are treated with care the dishes are elevated above the norm. Cornish cod, for example, is served with jerusalem artichokes, rainbow chard, cockles, trout roe and cider.

With many of the cosy rooms featuring views across Mount's Bay or out to sea, staying the night is seriously tempting.

Trencherman's tip

During warmer months, make a beeline for The Crabshack outdoor bar and kitchen. Enjoy seafood specials with a pint of craft beer or locally roasted speciality coffee from Yallah.

Chef Danny Garland | **3-course dinner from** £45 | **Seats** 65 | **Bedrooms** 14 | **Room rate from** £185

oldcoastguardhotel.co.uk | The Parade, Mousehole, Penzance, Cornwall, TR19 6PR | 01736 731222

2 Porthminster Beach Café

Shoreside suppers in St Ives

Perched on the white sands of Porthminster Beach, this multi-award-winning restaurant delivers seafood dishes and seascapes whose beauty is rivalled only by the art hanging in nearby Tate St Ives.

While so many restaurants in coastal destinations close their shutters in the winter months, this perennially popular spot bustles regardless of the season.

From daybreak to nightfall, vibrant dishes stream from the busy kitchen and land on tables in the pared-back dining room, where they're swiftly devoured. The heated outdoor terrace is also open all year for those wishing to dine with a salty breeze brushing their skin.

Chef-owner Mick Smith has long enjoyed a sterling reputation for his Asian- and Mediterranean-inspired cooking, and the restaurant's prestige has continued to climb since Ben Prior (formerly of Ben's Cornish Kitchen in Marazion) joined the team in 2023.

The seasoned chefs craft dishes based on the bounty of produce at their fingertips – from the freshest seafood and foraged coastal ingredients to garden-grown herbs and veggies.

Menus are switched up regularly, but a typical Porthminster supper could be hand-dived scallop crudo with ponzu mackerel and St Ives crab, followed by the (house favourite) fish curry comprising monkfish, market fish, tiger prawns, mussels and sweet potato, and culminating in a sweet finale of a strawberry and elderflower ice-cream sandwich.

Chefs Mick Smith and Ben Prior | **3-course dinner from** £50 | **Seats** 100

porthminstercafe.co.uk | Porthminster Beach, St Ives, Cornwall, TR26 2EB | 01736 795352

Award for Creativity and Innovation

Ugly Butterfly by Adam Handling

'Trencherman's is a fantastic celebration of the South West. We couldn't be prouder'

Tobie Heseltine, restaurant manager

Left to right: Tobie Heseltine and Connor Blades of Ugly Butterfly by Adam Handling with Dan Frost of Sharp's Brewery (award sponsor)

3 Ugly Butterfly by Adam Handling

Sustainable local luxury

Following the success of his pair of London restaurants (The Loch & the Tyne in Old Windsor and Michelin-starred Frog in Covent Garden), chef Adam Handling set his sights on the South West. The result? Ugly Butterfly, housed within the stunning Carbis Bay Estate.

With wraparound views of the crystal waters of Carbis Bay, Ugly Butterfly is a venue that promises to entice, surprise and delight thanks to a duo of chefs who aren't afraid to push the boundaries of the dining experience.

Adam works in synergy with executive chef Jamie Park to devise innovative five- and seven-course tasting menus that have a relentlessly sustainable aim: nothing goes to waste. Any leftover part of an ingredient is utilised elsewhere. The stems and tops of fruit and veg are used to form the basis of cocktails, while offcuts of meat are crafted into tasty bar snacks.

In 2023, Adam was crowned *Great British Menu* Champion of Champions and fans of the series will delight in the opportunity to sample his banquet-winning dessert, Food Fight. It features locally foraged Hayle strawberries with burnt butter 'mistake cake', long pepper custard and strawberry sorbet.

Trencherman's tip

Feast on Cornish turbot with mussels, courgette and basil while enjoying a view of the very waters from which your meal was caught.

Chef Jamie Park | **7-course tasting menu** £135 | **Seats** 65 | **EV charging**
uglybutterfly.co.uk | Carbis Bay, St Ives, Cornwall, TR26 2NP | 01736 805800

4 Kota Restaurant

Porthleven feasting with Asian flair

This flagship restaurant from Jude Kereama, *Great British Menu* veteran and recipient of the Award for Special Contribution at the Trencherman's Awards 2020, is the go-to for dynamic fusion dining in Porthleven.

Discerning foodies make the trip to sample Jude's three-AA-rosette menus, which major on seafood (Kota means 'shellfish' in Māori).

Standout dishes – such as kombu-cured weever fish, turnip and XO sauce, and gurnard cooked over coals paired with a brown crab sauce – utilise fresh local produce. They're inspired by a diverse mix of the chef's travels across the globe, his Cornish fishing village home and his Chinese-Malay and Māori heritage.

Small plates recently became a permanent fixture on the lunch menu, offering guests the opportunity to order as many (or as few) dishes as they like for leisurely grazing. Must-eats include Porthilly oysters doused in homemade beetroot vinegar, and deep-fried ox cheek and oyster croustillant with watercress emulsion and horseradish mayo.

Jude's menus are skilfully executed by newly appointed head chef Ross Sloan. A good friend of Jude, Ross was head chef at Kota a decade ago and made his comeback to this creative kitchen in late 2022.

Trencherman's tip

Take full advantage of the tasting menu wine pairings by staying in one of three harbour-view bedrooms above the restaurant. After a good night's sleep, swing by sister bar and kitchen Kota Kai (also in Porthleven) for a laid-back lunch.

Chef Ross Sloan | **4-course dinner from** £52.50 | **Seats** 36 | **Bedrooms** 3 | **Room rate from** £120

kotarestaurant.co.uk | Harbour Head, Porthleven, Helston, Cornwall, TR13 9JA | 01326 562407

5 The Cove Restaurant and Bar

This waterfront restaurant ticks all the boxes for lunch or dinner by the coast, combining exceptional dining and service with the beachy backdrop of Maenporth's golden sands and turquoise waters.

It's one of two Cornish restaurants in the Michael Caines Collection (sister to The Harbourside Refuge in Porthleven), and blends the chef's polished style with a casual feasting vibe to create a venue for all occasions – from family suppers to date nights and celebratory meals.

Steering the kitchen is group executive chef Stuart Shaw, who joined the Caines collective in 2022. With a wealth of experience from stints at prestigious spots such as Boodles, Savoy Grill and Le Manoir Aux Quat'Saisons, Stuart is committed to sourcing sustainably and locally.

Given the view of the briny blue from the dining room, fish is high on the must-try list. The all-day menu doesn't disappoint, delivering dishes like pan-fried fillet of Cornish hake with chorizo, parmentier potatoes, broccoli puree and salsa verde. For those celebrating, the tasting menu is a real treat and features signature Caines dishes such as sea bream ceviche with avocado, citrus vinaigrette and coriander oil.

Trencherman's tip

Dine alfresco year-round on a spacious terrace with heaters, blankets and a retractable roof. Indoors? Experience the glorious views across the beach to the Roseland Peninsula through the floor-to-ceiling windows.

Chef Michael Caines MBE | **3-course dinner from** £45 | **Seats** 80

thecovemaenporth.co.uk | Maenporth Beach, Falmouth, Cornwall, TR11 5HN | 01326 251136

6 St Michaels Resort

Feed body and soul in style

Leafy tropical gardens, two smart restaurants and a lush spa make this foodie resort in Falmouth a must-visit for those looking to feed both body and soul.

St Michaels' executive chef Darren Millgate is a great fan of produce grown and reared on Cornwall's soil or pulled from its waters, so his cooking showcases the county's freshest seasonal finds. His two-AA-rosette menus at Brasserie on the Bay include a 'Best of Local' selection featuring details on the provenance of dishes that have been built around a key ingredient.

In addition to the Brasserie, which specialises in ingredients cooked on the grill, the Garden Kitchen offers casual dining with wood-fired pizza and nutritious salads.

Guests will find further entertainment by wandering through luxuriant gardens, lazing in the largest hydrothermal pool in the South West, getting wrapped in seaweed in the spa and working up a sweat at the high-calibre fitness centre. Outdoor thrills include sea swimming and paddleboarding at Gylly Beach at the end of the drive.

Trencherman's tip

Experience a taste of the Cornish coast by ordering the half-shell, hand-dived scallops served with roasted garlic, seaweed butter and fresh lemon.

Chef Darren Millgate | **3-course dinner from** £45 | **Seats** 80
Bedrooms 92 | **Room rate from** £75 | **EV charging**

stmichaelsresort.com | Gyllyngvase Beach, Falmouth, Cornwall, TR11 4NB | 01326 312707

7 The Greenbank Hotel

Waterside feasting in Falmouth

Falmouth has been home to many hotels of note over the years, but none have stood the test of time like The Greenbank. Dating back to 1640 and first advertised as a hotel in 1831, this historic building overlooking the Fal Estuary has hosted many illustrious guests including Florence Nightingale and *The Wind in the Willows* author Kenneth Grahame.

While the hotel is steeped in history, the atmosphere is casual and contemporary. At its Water's Edge restaurant, head chef Bobby Southworth works alongside exec chef Nick Hodges to deliver creative dishes that showcase the finest Cornish ingredients. The restaurant is wrapped in glass to reveal stunning views over the water, so it's only natural that Bobby and Nick build their menus around the local fishermen's catch.

After dinner, head to the adjoining Water's Edge bar to watch the boats bobbing as you indulge in an inventive cocktail.

For a change of scene, head below deck to the hotel's pub, The Working Boat, to sink a local craft beer and tuck into Cornish-crab doorstop sandwiches or surf-and-turf burgers.

Experience a full gourmet getaway by booking one of the contemporary bedrooms. They make an excellent base from which to explore the National Maritime Museum Cornwall, Pendennis Castle and the South West Coast Path, all just a short stroll away.

Trencherman's tip

Upgrade to The Florence Suite to drink in the harbour views from a private balcony.

Chef Bobby Southworth | **3-course dinner from** £45 | **Seats** 60
Bedrooms 61 | **Room rate from** £129 | **EV charging**

greenbank-hotel.co.uk | Harbourside, Falmouth, Cornwall, TR11 2SR | 01326 312440

8 The Idle Rocks

Idyllic waterfront retreat

Whether you're sipping a cocktail on the harbour-view terrace, relishing the sunset over the water from your sea-view bedroom or watching a film in the 25-seater Hidden Cinema, The Idle Rocks is a great place to unwind.

The Relais & Châteaux hotel's waterfront location and exemplary hospitality are reason enough to visit, but in-the-know foodies flock for the inventive food offering from head chef Matt Haggath and team.

They've designed a menu that promises a culinary journey around Cornwall. It majors on seasonal flavours, with fresh ingredients sourced through carefully developed relationships with local suppliers, farmers and MSC-certified fishermen.

Signature dishes include St Mawes mackerel (caught within shouting distance) with romesco, hispi cabbage and sesame dressing, and roasted monkfish with girolles, black garlic, seaweed and cider sauce. Desserts are elegant yet unfussy – think strawberry and basil crémeux with yogurt, pistachio, matcha and clotted cream.

Trencherman's tip

For a gourmet getaway, book a room for the night. The decor takes inspiration from the stunning harbour views and oozes contemporary coastal style. It's a brilliant base from which to explore the tranquil Roseland Peninsula or take the ferry over to lively Falmouth. Or simply stay put – request a Grand Seaview Room with window-side tub in which to soak while watching sailing boats glide through the bay.

Chef Matthew Haggath | **3-course dinner from** £85 | **Seats** 50
Bedrooms 18 | **Room rate from** £265 | **EV charging**

idlerocks.com | Harbourside, St Mawes, Cornwall, TR2 5AN | 01326 270270

9 The Nare Hotel

Charming dining by the sea

With its English country-house charm and stonking sea views across the Roseland Peninsula, The Nare transports guests to a bygone era where G&Ts in the lounge and a stroll on the beach before dinner were standard.

The hotel hosts both a restaurant and a more formal dining room, each of which showcases the finest Cornish produce from land and sea.

The two-AA-rosette Quarterdeck restaurant's yacht-themed decor matches its menu, which features local lobster and decadent seafood platters. There are also options from the surrounding countryside, such as succulent fillet of Cornish beef or tenderloin of pork wrapped in pancetta.

More formal dining and a daily changing menu can be found in The Dining Room.

Expect starched powder-blue tablecloths, silver service and trollies wheeled to your table brimming with hors d'oeuvres, desserts and cheese. This is the place to be for those who enjoy donning their glad rags and revelling in impeccable service.

The Nare's Sunday lunches are elegant affairs too. Begin with an aperitif and canapés in the lounge before taking your seat at a table overlooking the ocean.

Trencherman's tip

For a romantic adventure, hotel guests can book The Nare's motor launch to enjoy a picnic on the waves.

Chef Nick Lawrie | **Seats** 60 | **Bedrooms** 40 | **Room rate from** £312 | **EV charging**

narehotel.co.uk | Carne Beach, Veryan-in-Roseland, Cornwall, TR2 5PF | 01872 501111

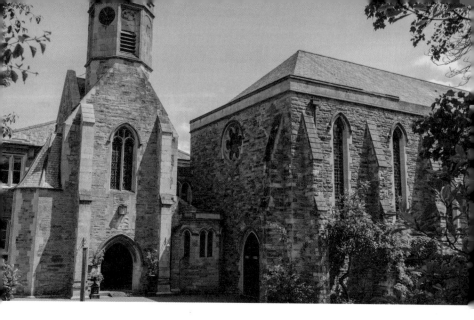

10 The Alverton Hotel

Historic luxury in the Cornish capital

The Alverton is a hidden treasure in the city of Truro, tucked away at the top of a winding drive and surrounded by mature gardens. It feels a world away from the bustle of the city, when in fact it's only a ten-minute stroll from its centre.

The Grade II*-listed hotel's riches are revealed at every turn: on discovery of its history as a private residence turned convent; when unwinding on the sunny terrace with an exquisite cocktail in hand; and on waking in one of the luxuriously refurbished bedrooms and suites.

However, the true jewel is to be found in the elegant cooking that comes courtesy of a skilled team led by Ollie Wyatt and overseen by executive chef Nick Hodges. The seasonally focused menu features the best of land and sea, with Ollie's pick of the Cornish daybboats' catch (such as whole Cornish sole with grape vermouth velouté and samphire) rubbing shoulders with duck leg scrumpet served with fennel, pistachio, orange and white-miso mayonnaise.

Locally foraged accompaniments elevate seasonal flavours to centre stage in the likes of the spring flowerpot of sugared filo, chocolate soil, elderflower curd and berries.

Trencherman's tip

The Alverton hosts a number of events throughout the year, including live music Summer Sessions on the terrace and Taste of Truro suppers.

Chef Ollie Wyatt | **3-course dinner from** £45 | **Seats** 60
Bedrooms 53 | **Room rate from** £119 | **EV charging**

thealverton.co.uk | Tregolls Road, Truro, Cornwall, TR1 1ZQ | 01872 276633

11 The Barley Sheaf at Gorran

Sustainable dining in a classic country-pub setting

Chef proprietor Tim Kendall and team have upped their eco status this year by reducing plastic waste, implementing energy-efficient practices and stepping up their local sourcing ethos. It's all part of their vision to create the perfect community pub – one that not only serves villagers and visitors but also contributes positively to the local environment.

Tim took over The Barley Sheaf in February 2020 and, despite the difficult timing, has built a cracking reputation for delicious and well-executed dishes that reflect the surrounding seascape and countryside.

Before pursuing this first solo venture, Tim worked with some of the best chefs in the industry including Paul Ainsworth, Chris Eden and Guy Owen. At The Barley Sheaf he works alongside head chef Dan Hyams, and the two seamlessly blend experienced cooking with the relaxed pub setting. The result is a menu that includes well-crafted crowd-pleasers such as St Ewe scotch egg with spiced pork and curry mayo, and ponzu-glazed Newlyn mackerel with horseradish sauce, pickled cucumber, dashi tomato, 'nduja and pork skin.

The country inn is decorated in earthy heritage tones with slate flooring and local artwork on the walls – smart enough for occasion dining yet so easygoing that no one would raise an eyebrow if you turned up with a four-legged friend in tow.

Trencherman's tip

The pub runs regular live music events and themed parties – details can usually be found on the website.

Chef Dan Hyams | 3-course dinner from £30 | Seats 55

thebarleysheafgorran.co.uk | Gorran Churchtown, St Austell, Cornwall, PL26 6HN | 01726 843330

12 Appleton's Bar & Restaurant

A taste of Italy in Fowey

'*Non si vive di solo pane*', translating as '*you don't live on bread alone*', is an apt motto for this Fowey eatery, which excels at Italian-inspired cuisine made from artisan Cornish produce.

From the moment guests are ushered through the door to the point where they put down their dessert spoons, they're made to feel like part of the family in this relaxed yet expertly run restaurant. Overseeing front of house is Lyndsey Appleton, one half of the husband-and-wife team who own and run the restaurant. Andy Appleton heads up the kitchen, knocking out first-rate plates that draw on his passion for classic Italian cooking with a modern edge.

Expect to find the finest Cornish seafood paired with heavenly homemade pasta in dishes such as squid-ink linguine with Cornish crab, chilli and fennel seed pangrattato, and mafaldine and Cornish lobster ragu with lemon gremolata. Meanwhile, desserts such as chocolate pannacotta and an Italian-leaning drinks list (with wines from most regions of the country) allow a surrendering of the senses to the full continental dining experience.

Before leaving, grab a bag of Andy's handcrafted pasta from the in-house deli to take home.

Trencherman's tip

Struggling to get a reservation? The countertop seating overlooking the bar isn't bookable, so walk-ins might just get lucky.

Chef Andy Appleton | **3-course dinner from £34** | **Seats** 60

appletonsrestaurant.com | 19 Fore Street, Fowey, Cornwall, PL23 1AH | 01872 228738

13 The Old Quay House Hotel

Fowey's hidden waterside haunt

Once a refuge for sailors, the present-day incarnation of this whitewashed Victorian building is a fabulous find for tourists heading to Fowey for sea air, smart dining and a well-curated bar list.

With its yachty vibe and winding narrow streets, the pretty town offers excellent pottering, shopping and strolling opportunities. And, being on the South West Coast Path, a serious stomp is also in the offing.

However the day is spent, there's nowhere like The Old Quay House Hotel's waterside terrace for summer-evening dining. Book a table to feast on locally sourced, quality seafood such as pan-roasted cod served with wild-garlic potato cake, oyster mushroom and confit leeks. And, while diving into a dish of the freshest fish and shellfish may feel like the only option in this location, piscatorial delights share menu space with West Country meats, cheeses and veggies.

Save room for pud, too, as the likes of set lemon cream with pink rhubarb, oat crumb and rhubarb granita are hard to resist.

Trencherman's tip

Given that the hotel houses a small but elegant Champagne bar, the sensible option is to plump for an overnight stay in one of the bespoke bedrooms. Spend a peaceful night being lulled by the gentle clinking of the boats beyond the window, before starting the following morning with a gourmet breakfast of the highest order.

Chef Richard Massey | **3-course dinner from** £45 | **Seats** 28
Bedrooms 13 | **Room rate from** £147.50

theoldquayhouse.com | 28 Fore Street, Fowey, Cornwall, PL23 1AQ | 01726 833302

14 Talland Bay Hotel

Escapist coastal dining

The epitome of luxury, Talland Bay is a secluded coastal retreat for those wishing to experience the true spirit of Cornwall, away from the crowds.

It's also a foodie paradise, thanks to the creative genius of head chef Glen Merriot and his team. The à la carte menu may wear its French influence on its sleeve in dishes like fillet of beef with roast Roscoff onion, truffle pommes anna and a blue cheese and mustard croquette, but the ingredients are determinedly local – like the Philip Warren beef, which is reared on rich Cornish pastures.

For those seeking an immersive evening, the nine-course tasting experience with wine pairings is a must. Each impeccably plated dish is explained by the team on presentation, showcasing the provenance of your meal as you dine.

It's quite possible you won't want to leave after all this exquisite wining and dining. Fortunately, accommodation is available for every taste, from sea-view and dog-friendly rooms to garden cottages and a self-catering bungalow.

Trencherman's tip

In summer, after feasting in the restaurant or sea-view conservatory, there's no better place to soak up the evening rays than the lush subtropical gardens. For perfection, pair the experience with a Talland Bay No.1 gin, crafted with pines and botanicals grown on the grounds.

Chef Glen Merriot | **3-course dinner from** £38 | **Seats** 42
Bedrooms 20 | **Room rate from** £220 | **EV charging**

tallandbayhotel.co.uk | Porthallow, Looe, Cornwall, PL13 2JB | 01503 272667

15 Scarlet Hotel

Eco sanctuary on the coast

It's all about balance at Scarlet Hotel: not the ripped-abs type demonstrated by the surfers carving through the waves beyond the balconies but in the delicate harmony and tension between ethical sustainability and utter indulgence.

Scarlet was groundbreaking when it launched as an adults-only boutique eco-hotel in 2009. It continues to lead the field, providing a sophisticated yet sustainable experience where you can luxuriate in low-impact lazing and feasting. Guests enjoy captivating Atlantic views from every room – even some of the bathrooms.

Head chef Jack Clayton's passion for seafood and sustainability marries perfectly with the environmental reputation of the hotel. Having previously achieved three AA rosettes and two Bib Gourmands during his career in

the East Midlands, his philosophy centres on showcasing the journey of individual ingredients, which are largely seasonal, foraged and local. Highlights of Jack's new Cornish menu include sea-trout pastrami with horseradish, cucumber, mustard seeds and soda bread, and whole john dory with leek, parsley, lemon butter sauce and herring eggs.

Trencherman's tip

Bliss out with a bespoke treatment at the clifftop spa. It boasts equal eco creds to the rest of the hotel thanks to its bromine-filtered indoor pool, outdoor natural reed pool and cedar-wood barrel sauna.

Chef Jack Clayton | **3-course dinner from** £60 | **Seats** 56
Bedrooms 37 | **Room rate from** £250 | **EV charging**

scarlethotel.co.uk | Tredragon Road, Mawgan Porth, Cornwall, TR8 4DQ | 01637 861800

16 Bedruthan Hotel & Spa
Creative outpost on a clifftop

Bedruthan is the sister hotel and neighbour of the grown-ups-only Scarlet Hotel, and shares its stylish vibe. A swish spa for adults is paired with plenty to keep kids entertained, while everyone will enjoy the quality cooking.

Its two popular restaurants have recently been refreshed and rebranded. Plant, Fish and Grill at The Wild Café is a friendly, brightly coloured clifftop cafe serving natural, nourishing fare which will appeal to all the family.

Ogo ('cave' in Cornish) replaces The Herring, and it's here that head chef George Richardson creates a line-up of dishes that puts Cornwall's abundant produce front and centre. It's a veritable feast of sea, garden and field, and a showcase of hyper-seasonal sustainable dining.

Begin with a sharing selection for the table, including the likes of citrus-cured sea trout taco and duck liver parfait, followed by steamed Cornish brill with Champagne, mussels and sea herbs. Local suppliers include Padstow Kitchen Garden, Primrose Herd, Mora Farm in the Fowey Valley and Trewithen Dairy.

The hotel has been in the same family for over 60 years, with architecture evoking California and furnishings imported from Denmark long before Scandi style became popular.

The golden sands of Mawgan Porth beach are a mere stone's throw away. The hotel is dog-friendly and canine companions will love a bracing walk along the South West Coast Path to view the famous Bedruthan Steps rock formation.

Chef George Richardson | **3-course dinner from** £50 | **Seats** 76 (Ogo), 170 (Plant, Fish and Grill)
Bedrooms 110 | **Room rate from** £90 | **EV charging**

bedruthan.com | Mawgan Porth, Cornwall, TR4 4BU | 01637 861200

17 **The Seafood Restaurant**

Stein's Padstow classic

With its winning mix of smart-casual dining, ultra-fresh local seafood and global wines, Rick and Jill Stein's flagship restaurant is a longstanding classic on the South West dining scene.

Join the discerning pilgrims who journey to Padstow to sample Stein favourites such as the gloriously messy Singapore chilli crab or Indonesian seafood curry of cod, monkfish and prawns. Dishes change frequently depending on what produce head chef Pete Murt gets delivered to his kitchen door, so there's always something fresh to try.

Those looking to push the boat out should sample the tronçon of turbot with hollandaise sauce. Served in the English style, it's Rick's all-time favourite dish.

Dining at a table in the restaurant is delightful but, if you're only swinging by for a bite and a glass of wine, take the opportunity to perch at the zinc bar and watch the restaurant in action.

For the full Stein experience book one of the upstairs guestrooms, many of which have enjoyed a stylish makeover this year.

Trencherman's tip

The three-course set lunch menu, available for £30 on weekdays from October to May, is fabulous value if you're after a daytime dining experience.

Chef Pete Murt | **3-course dinner from** £45 | **Seats** 130 | **Bedrooms** 16 | **Room rate from** £170

rickstein.com | Riverside, Padstow, Cornwall, PL28 8BY | 01841 532700

THE
eco
LAUNDRY
that doesn't cost the earth

Providing a sustainable future for the laundry industry

ecolaundry.co.uk

18 The St Enodoc Hotel

Tasting menus in boutique setting

There's an authentically personal feel to this family-owned hotel nestled in the hills that line the Camel Estuary. Each of its 21 bedrooms is individually styled and furnished, local artworks colour the walls and service is warm and friendly – just a few of the reasons why so many guests return year after year.

St Enodoc's idyllic setting, outdoor heated pool and Elemis spa may make it an attractive getaway destination, but it's the hotel's two restaurants that have earned it a place in the upper echelons of the South West hospitality elite.

The hotel has a history of having great head chefs, and when Guy Owen took on the leading role in 2020 he was determined to elevate the dining experience further. He succeeded: Karrek – St Enodoc's more formal restaurant – garnered three AA rosettes on its first appearance in the guide.

Open for dinner Thursday to Saturday, Karrek has a tasting-menu-only offering from which guests can choose a six- or nine-course experience. The series of innovative dishes blurs the boundary between food and art, delighting diners with complex techniques, flavours and presentation.

Much of the produce for Karrek and its more relaxed sister restaurant, The St Enodoc Brasserie, is sourced from the on-site kitchen garden and the hotel's farm in neighbouring Devon.

Trencherman's tip

In summer, join the weekly barbecue lunch on the terrace.

Chef Guy Owen | **3-course dinner from** £35 | **Seats** 46 | **Bedrooms** 21 | **Room rate from** £175

enodoc-hotel.co.uk | Rock Road, Wadebridge, Cornwall, PL27 6LA | 01208 863394

Award for Special Contribution

Nathan Outlaw

'Trencherman's is one of those guides you want to get into as a chef, so it's amazing to receive this'

Nathan Outlaw

Left to right: Mark Hix (host) and Nathan Outlaw
with Nick Farrant of PKF Francis Clark (award sponsor)

19 Outlaw's New Road

Fresh moves at New Road

Nathan Outlaw's eponymous restaurant in Port Isaac continues to reshape its offering for diners keen to experience the acclaimed chef's cooking. However, one thing remains the same: Outlaw's is still *the* place to delight in excellently executed fish dishes.

At New Road, Nathan cooks the kind of food he loves to eat, namely quality local seafood prepared in a way that lets the ingredients do the talking. A revised evening dining experience means the restaurant now exclusively offers a seafood tasting menu, which pioneers innovative ways of preparing and cooking the exceptional Cornish catch.

Expect dishes like baked turbot with velvet crab sauce, lobster with orange and basil risotto, and raw scallop with smoked roe. Despite the move to a more informal style of dining, New Road has retained its Michelin star and placed sixth in the list of the UK's best restaurants in *The Good Food Guide*.

Daytime diners are in for something special, too. To mark 20 years since Nathan opened The Black Pig (his first restaurant in Cornwall), the chef has launched an à la carte lunch menu honouring his favourite dishes from the past two decades.

Trencherman's tip

The recent unveiling of Outlaw's Guest House offers the chance for an exclusive foodie escape. Stay in one of nine bedrooms in the refurbished Victorian building or one of two self-catering coastal retreats, all just moments from the harbour.

Chef Nathan Outlaw | **Seafood tasting menu** £175 | **Seats** 20 | **EV charging**

outlaws.co.uk | 6 New Road, Port Isaac, Cornwall, PL29 3SB | 01208 880896

20 The Godolphin Hotel & Restaurant

Boho bolthole by the beach

A mere pebble's skim from the beach and with views out to St Michael's Mount, this boutique hotel in Marazion is in an enviable location. Its spectacular setting makes The Godolphin an ideal base for gourmets who want to explore the tidal island (which lies just half a mile off the coast) before retreating to the comfort of the hotel for dinner at its Shutters restaurant.

The dining room's floor-to-ceiling windows provide a mesmerising vista of the mystical castle and the tide lapping the shore. Watching white-tipped waves while perusing a menu awash with fish and shellfish should rouse the appetite for seafood, and satiation can be found in dishes like South Coast sea trout with braised baby gem, Fowey mussels and crab, and samphire.

Menus are created around local ingredients including seafood caught by Cornish dayboats and meat and veg from nearby farms. This quality produce is crafted into classic dishes that emphasise the natural flavours of land and sea.

The decor is as slick as the cooking, with a bohemian-chic vibe and subtle nods to all things nautical. Funky finishing touches include rattan peacock chairs, Berber-style rugs and jazzy lampshades.

Trencherman's tip

After checking in – and experiencing the jungle-themed reception complete with lush houseplants, ornamental animals and wild wallpaper – head to the bar for a craft cocktail or simply curl up with a brew in the porthole windowsill of your bedroom.

3-course dinner from £46 | Seats 80 | Bedrooms 10 | Room rate from £180

thegodolphin.com | West End, Mount's Bay, Marazion, Cornwall, TR17 0EN | 01736 888510

21 Source Kitchen

Globally inspired Cornish fare

St Ives has long been a cultural and gastronomic magnet, attracting visitors from far and wide for its beaches, galleries and fantastic dining.

The Digey is an archetypal Cornish fishing village alleyway and is home to Source Kitchen. The restaurant is run by husband-and-wife team Stephen and Sophie Holloway, who met while training to be chefs. Their menus are inspired by their travels and love of European and Middle Eastern cuisines but are executed using the best local produce, resulting in an intimate yet informal dining experience of beautiful and unfussy dishes.

Menus change with the seasons and capitalise on the latest dayboat and line-caught (never trawled) fish, and meat from regenerative farms, sourced and aged by Philip Warren Butchers.

Guests are invited to share a selection of plates, sent from the open kitchen as and when they're ready. Cornish oysters come au naturel, à la mignonette (with shallot vinegar) or Thai style with nahm jim dressing, while St Austell Bay mussels are served with Duchy Charcuterie 'nduja and Cornish cream.

A wine list of UK and European wines includes six English varieties served by the glass. And if you're a cocktail fan, don't leave without trying a post-dinner Liquid Dessert: a Cornish Espresso Martini made using Fowey Valley Cornish Vodka and Cornico coffee roasted near Wadebridge.

Trencherman's tip

Catch a true taste of the terroir by opting for a plate of ultra-fresh dressed Cornish crab, served with lemon mayo, pickled cucumber and crostini.

Chef Stephen Holloway | **Dinner from** £50 | **Seats** 32

sourcekitchen.co.uk | 6 The Digey, St Ives, Cornwall, TR26 1HR | 01736 799487

22 Hotel Meudon

Sub-tropical paradise

Sitting on the terrace of this hotel and restaurant, swathed in nine acres of sub-tropical gardens and looking out to sea, it's hard to believe you're only a few miles from the busy hubbub of Falmouth.

Hotel Meudon's location is one of its best attributes. It's within walking distance of the foodie town and some of the area's best beaches (follow the coast path that snakes past its garden gate to reach Maenporth and Swanpool, and eventually Falmouth) but it also feels incredibly peaceful and private.

The recently refurbished hotel in Mawnan Smith is a superb base for a gourmet getaway on Cornwall's south coast. Newly appointed head chef David Waters worked with Nathan Outlaw in Port Isaac before making the move to Hotel Meudon, so diners can expect a strong showing of fish and shellfish when they eat here.

While his menus are rooted in local ingredients (David has plans to grow fruit, veg and herbs in the hotel gardens), the chef takes inspiration from south-east Asia.

'My partner is from Thailand so we eat a lot of Thai food at home. I love bold flavours, but keep things simple and don't overcomplicate dishes,' says David.

Trencherman's tip

Make time for a pre-dinner drink at Freddie's Bar. Its crimson-hued walls, rich velvet furnishings and burnt gold features create an inviting setting for cocktail hour.

Chef David Waters | **3-course dinner from** £49 | **Seats** 60
Bedrooms 29 | **Room rate from** £119 | **EV charging**
meudon.co.uk | Mawnan Smith, Falmouth, Cornwall, TR11 5HT | 01326 250541

23 Hooked on the Rocks

Casual seafood by the beach

Nothing captures the spirit of Cornish summer quite like a dip in its azure waters followed by a plate of lusciously fresh seafood. It's this very experience that gourmets can enjoy at Hooked on the Rocks, a stone's throw from the shore of Falmouth's Swanpool Beach.

Located on the cliffside with views out to sea, it's the perfect spot for lunch or dinner alfresco. The menu centres around local, sustainably sourced seafood and features the likes of crab and lobster (caught just eight miles down the coast), Falmouth Bay scallops, and daily fish specials from Newlyn market.

If you can't decide on a single dish, indulge in the hot shellfish platter for two, which features scallops, prawns, cockles, clams and mussels. Other highlights include shell-on wild prawns with 'nduja butter or whole baked market fish.

A simple wine list focuses on small family-run vineyards practising sustainable viticulture. Alternatively, pair your pick of the day's seafood with a South West tipple from the likes of Loveday Gin in Falmouth, High Point non-alcoholic spirits, or Sharp's Brewery beer and cider. There's a good cocktail list too, which includes a knockout Cornish Negroni.

The team recently launched a partnership with The National Lobster Hatchery, which helps conserve local lobster populations. For every lobster sold in the restaurant, a donation is made to the Padstow charity.

Trencherman's tip

Sun shining? Dine on the sea-view terrace, or under the heated awning area on cooler days.

Chef Jack Frame | **3-course dinner from** £50 | **Seats** 45 inside, 60 outside

hookedontherocksfalmouth.com | Swanpool, Falmouth, Cornwall, TR11 5BG | 01326 311886

24 The Watch House

Laid-back feasting in St Mawes

The smart south-coast village of St Mawes is blessed with more than its fair share of excellent dining options, but for joyfully casual cooking in a relaxed and attractive setting this is your go-to.

Jay Rayner recently singled out The Watch House as one of the best value places to eat out on the British coast and it's easy to see why. It's the kind of place where you can rock up straight from the beach, sand between toes, and tuck into a lunch or supper of classic moules frites, seafood spaghetti or the freshest dayboat catch.

There's no fuss or standing on ceremony, just straight-up delicious local produce prepared by head chef Brad King and served in a laid-back, family-friendly environment.

Working alongside chef founder Will Gould, Brad is a passionate proponent of supporting local artisan suppliers, so you'll find delivery vans pulling up early each morning from top-notch producers such as Da Bara Bakery, Philip Warren Butchers and Harbour Brewing. Treleavens Luxury Cornish Ice Cream provides the sweet scoops while Rodda's delivers the clotted cream.

Fancy eating supper on the beach as the sun sets over the water? Get The Watch House's award-winning fish and chip supper to go – just don't forget a picnic rug.

Trencherman's tip

Those dining in who are looking to push the boat out should order the roasted shellfish platter: a smorgasbord of half-shell scallops, tiger prawns, mussels and crab claws, care of Wing of St Mawes and Matthew Stevens Cornish Fish.

Chef Brad King | **3-course dinner from** £35 | **Seats** 70

watchhousestmawes.co.uk | 1 The Square, St Mawes, Truro, Cornwall, TR2 5DJ | 01326 270038

25 The Rising Sun

Community spirit in the city

It's no easy task striking the balance between polished dining pub and a home-from-home for locals looking to put the world to rights over a pint. Yet The Rising Sun's owners, Tom and Katie Hannon, have achieved it in spades.

Truro doesn't suffer the tourist fluctuations of its coastal counterparts, so the pub draws a year-round following of loyal locals. You can understand why they're chuffed to call this their local: Tom and Katie have spent nine years transforming it from run-down boozer to dining destination with a zero-waste ethos and bundles of community spirit.

Chef Tom's creativity and experience are evidenced in evolving menus that utilise the best of nearby land and sea. Relationships with local suppliers were established from day one, resulting in longstanding alliances which ensure the kitchen is supplied with

fish fresh from Cornish waters, microgreens snipped that morning, and quality meats reared on South West soil.

From this bounty, Tom crafts pleasing seasonal dishes like scallops with salt-baked celeriac, apple and hazelnuts, and West Country duck with orange-glazed carrots, sprouting broccoli, parmentier potatoes and pomegranate jus.

There are tasty developments brewing behind the bar, too. Look out for the selection of team-favourite cocktails as well as a paired cigar and craft spirits list.

Trencherman's tip

Thoughtful touches make a meal at The Rising Sun a memorable experience. Opt for steak and choose a weapon of choice from a case of bespoke knives, made in collaboration with Pareusi in St Agnes.

Chef Tom Hannon | **3-course dinner from** £27 | **Seats** 40

therisingsuntruro.co.uk | Mitchell Hill, Truro, Cornwall, TR1 1ED | 01872 240003

26 Pennypots Restaurant at The Falmouth Arms

Nostalgia-packed dining

In 1993, chef Kevin Viner made history when he earned Cornwall its first Michelin star at Pennypots in Blackwater, an accolade he retained at the restaurant for eight years. Three decades on, he has returned to his roots and relaunched Pennypots within The Falmouth Arms, his rural Ladock inn.

Since taking over The Falmouth Arms in 2019, husband-and-wife team Kevin and Jill have restored the former coaching inn, enhancing the character of its crooked walls and beamed ceilings with their own unique touches. It's where Kevin delights diners with seasonal menus that condense his immense repertoire into a handful of beautifully crafted, classic dishes.

In this new chapter for the inn, Kevin is revisiting the refined French dishes that helped him gain – and retain – Michelin success.

Wednesday to Saturday, guests can indulge in nostalgic compilations such as twice-baked West Country cheese soufflé, loin of Cornish venison with spiced pears, armagnac prunes and bitter chocolate jus, and chocolate temptation with garott cherries and hazelnut sorbet. On Sundays, however, The Falmouth Arms resumes its pub guise and serves a cracking Sunday lunch.

Trencherman's tip

Make the most of the experience by booking one of the cosy guestrooms and indulging in the excellent wine pairings.

Chef Kevin Viner | **3-course dinner from** £45 | **Seats** 40 | **Bedrooms** 4 | **Room rate from** £100
falmoutharms.com | Ladock, Cornwall, TR2 4PG | 01726 882319

27 Edie's

Family flair

Tucked away in the coastal resort of Carlyon Bay near St Austell, Edie's is a family affair. Cornishman Nigel Brown is in the kitchen, while his wife Kelly runs front of house and their eponymous daughter Edie makes mixology magic behind the bar.

Nigel spent 20 years cheffing with culinary luminaries such as Raymond Blanc at Le Manoir aux Quat'Saisons and Bill Granger in Sydney, before bringing his well-honed skills home. Guests can take a pew in the raised seating area overlooking the open kitchen to watch as he transforms local ingredients into flavourful combinations. The result is unfussy modern British dishes that reflect Nigel's French training (his soufflés, both savoury and sweet, are the stuff of legend).

Fresh fish is prominent on the seasonal menu, with the likes of gilt-head bream, halibut, red mullet and Cornish mackerel regularly featured. For sweet-toothed diners, the dessert of honey pannacotta with cereal-milk ice cream and peanut butter fudge is a must-try.

Dishes can be paired with wines from an extensive list that spans the globe. Beers, gins and vodkas in the well-stocked bar are exclusively Cornish.

Kelly has a wealth of experience in managing high-profile restaurants and is dedicated to creating a warm welcome and efficient service. The decor is relaxed with whitewashed brick walls, eclectic art and shelves full of cookbooks which guests are encouraged to flick through to whet their appetite for the feast to come.

Trencherman's tip

Northern soul and old-school funk provide a soundtrack in pleasing counterpoint to the contemporary dining.

Chef Nigel Brown | **3-course dinner from** £32 | **Seats** 42

edies.restaurant | 10 Beach Road, Carlyon Bay, St Austell, Cornwall, PL25 3PH | 01726 813888

28 The Sardine Factory

Sustainable seafood on the harbour

In the 19th century, Looe's Sardine Factory did exactly what it says on the tin: when fishermen shouted '*Hevva!*', it meant shoals of pilchards (known locally as Cornish sardines) had been sighted, and the boats would bring in the catch for processing and canning.

Chef-owner Ben Palmer had cherished a dream of opening a restaurant in his hometown, and in July 2018 he transformed this historic harbourside building into an 80-cover restaurant. Ben's passion in the kitchen has bagged him a number of awards, including a Michelin Bib Gourmand.

He works closely with head chef Charlie Walters, and together they specialise in creating sustainable fish dishes using produce from Looe's fish market (located directly opposite the restaurant). The dayboats' bounty is crafted into the likes of spiced stone bass accompanied by kachumber salad, lime yogurt and summer vegetable bhaji, and creamy local lobster risotto with tomatoes and basil. Of course, there are also the titular sardines, which are served simply with seaweed, lemon and garlic butter.

If raw seafood floats your boat, pick the tuna sashimi with mango, yuzu, sesame and puffed wild rice, or Porthilly oysters fresh from north Cornwall, served with Tabasco, jalapeño salsa and shallot vinegar.

Trencherman's tip

Take the scenic route to lunch along the Looe Valley branchline, one of the UK's most tranquil railway lines, which teems with wildlife – keep your eyes peeled for herons.

Chef Ben Palmer | **3-course dinner from** £25 | **Seats** 80

thesardinefactorylooe.com | The Quay, West Looe, Cornwall, PL13 2BX | 01503 770262

29 Fistral Beach Hotel and Spa

Grown-ups-only glamour

After a year dedicated to seeking out the best local producers and refining menus, in April 2023 the team at this chic hotel and restaurant were delighted to be awarded a second AA rosette.

Head chef Daniel Kerr has spent much of his career in Cornwall so knows exactly how to make seasonal Cornish ingredients sing. The five-course tasting menu (with optional wine flight) at the ocean-facing Dune Restaurant is the best way to sample his ambitious cooking. Explore culinary creations such as crab and prawn tortellini, monkfish loin with lentil dal and pickled carrots, and Fox Hill lamb with purple sprouting broccoli.

The surfy hotel has a luxury resort vibe thanks to its incredible views, contemporary styling and rock-star extras, so there's no compromise if you swap the south of France for the Cornish coast. Overlooking Newquay's sweeping Fistral Beach, the bar and restaurant's panoramic windows offer guests rolling coverage of surfers riding the waves below.

After a relaxing day of pampering in the Fistral Spa, kick off the evening with drinks in the Bay Bar. The experienced team, who scooped Best Bar List at the Trencherman's Awards 2022, serve signature cocktails such as The Hugo (a concoction of St-Germain Elderflower Liqueur, mint leaves, fresh lime, Prosecco and soda) as well as local craft beers.

Trencherman's tip

The vegan menu goes above and beyond to provide plant-based diners with creative options like salt-baked heritage beetroot tartlet with dukkah spice and herb salad.

Chef Daniel Kerr | **3-course dinner from** £45 | **Seats** 50
Bedrooms 71 | **Room rate from** £175 | **EV charging**

fistralbeachhotel.co.uk | Esplanade Road, Newquay, Cornwall, TR7 1PT | 01637 852221

Best Trencherman's Restaurant

Prawn on the Lawn

'It's been ten years since we started our business; this award feels like a massive anniversary present'

Rick Toogood, chef-owner

Left to right: Eddie Thomson (head chef at Barnaby's at Trevibban Mill), Colin Putt of Dole (award sponsor) and Rick Toogood of Prawn on the Lawn

30 Prawn on the Lawn

Creative seafood-centred small plates

Prawn on the Lawn may be one of Cornwall's most notable seafood restaurants, but it actually started out in 2013 as a tiny fishmonger and seafood bar in Islington. The original venue was such a hit that founders Rick and Katie Toogood decided to open a second site at the source of their impeccable produce: Padstow.

The POTL team kicked off their tenth-anniversary year with a bang when they picked up the Best Restaurant gong at the Trencherman's Awards 2023.

The menus at the Padstow restaurant are updated daily and dictated by what Cornish fishermen land each morning, so no two visits to this bijou seafood bar are ever quite the same. Working closely with new head chef James Lean (former head chef Eddie Thomson has moved up the road to sister restaurant Barnaby's), Rick favours sustainable fish and shellfish species and supplements the day's catch with hyper-fresh veg from the restaurant's own raised beds and produce from Ross Geach of Padstow Kitchen Garden.

Delicious dishes – such as hake with truffle oil, parmesan, cauliflower and porcini crumb; monkfish with North African marinade and herb salad; and lemon sole with 'nduja and tarragon – are complemented by local wines from Trevibban Mill (just a stone's throw away) and beers from Padstow Brewing Company.

As the restaurant is rather small, the team often host summer residencies at other local venues. Previous pop-ups have included Barnaby's at Trevibban Mill (now a permanent venue) and Prawn on the Farm at Trerethern Farm.

Chefs Rick Toogood and James Lean | **3-course dinner from** £50 | **Seats** 25

prawnonthelawn.com | 11 Duke Street, Padstow, Cornwall, PL28 8AB | 01841 532223

31 The Rising Sun Inn
Creative Cornish fare

This traditional 18th-century pub in the shadow of brooding Bodmin Moor captivates with an enticing menu, a fascinating past and striking surroundings.

Tim and Terri Kendall have garnered a well-earned reputation for running an unpretentious pub which not only serves quality food crafted from local ingredients but also doubles as an excellent base for exploring the county's inner heartlands. The pair have form when it comes to doing dining pubs well: they took over The Barley Sheaf in Gorran Haven in 2020, then expanded their portfolio with this north Cornwall venture in 2022.

Chef-owner Tim began his career at Rick Stein's The Seafood Restaurant in Padstow, and spent two years in London working with such luminaries as Michel Roux Jr and Marcus Wareing. At The Rising Sun,

he works with head chef Simon Davies (a former Nathan Outlaw apprentice) to lead a talented kitchen team.

Their menu offers 'traditional Cornish fare that embraces innovative twists'. That results in dishes such as saffron arancini with truffle mayo, chased by braised beef featherblade with smoked mash and red wine sauce, followed by queen of puddings lavished with rhubarb and orange.

Dogs are welcome in the bar and garden. In summer, guests can chill out with good food and drink at the regular outdoor Acoustic Sundays sessions.

Trencherman's tip

Don't fancy the drive home? Bag a free camping pitch when you eat in the restaurant.

Chef Tim Kendall | **3-course dinner from** £40 | **Seats** 60 | **Bedrooms** 3 | **Room rate from** £120

therisingsuninn.co.uk | Altarnun, Launceston, Cornwall, PL15 7SN | 01566 86636

32 Potters

Fish feasting in Bude

An exciting new development for this much-loved restaurant in Bude is a pivot to a more relaxed bistro-style menu, with seafood front and centre.

Chef Oly Clarke's menus maximise on Cornwall's super-fresh fishy bounty, with a smattering of meat and veg options thrown in.

Sharing plates of St Ives smoked mackerel pâté with pickles and sourdough, wild whitebait with marie rose sauce, and Atlantic Fungi mushroom arancini with truffle mayo tease proceedings. However, the main attraction is Potters' upmarket fish and chips, in which fillets of cod, haddock or hake are fried to crisp perfection.

Tandoori Cornish monkfish with coriander yogurt and red onion will also appeal to the piscatorially inclined, while southern fried chicken served with fried egg, honey and a bacon and chive waffle has proved a consistent crowd-pleaser. There's a daily specials board too, which showcases the day's catch along with fresh seasonal produce.

Pair the briny feast with a tipple from Potters' extensive drinks menu. Post-dinner cocktail? Plump for a classic Negroni, given a Cornish twist with Bude Gin.

Trencherman's tip

For those who fancy fish and chips by the sea, Potters offers a takeaway menu featuring family-friendly chip shop favourites.

Chef Oly Clarke | **3-course dinner from** £35 | **Seats** 30

pottersbude.co.uk | 2 Lansdown Road, Bude, Cornwall, EX23 8BH | 01288 358466

Devon

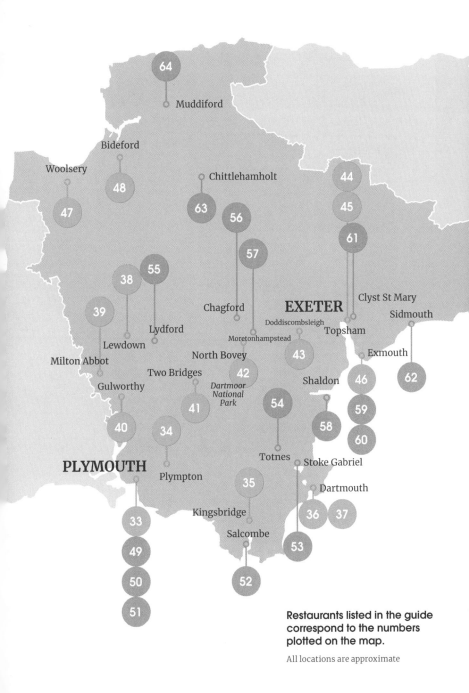

Muddiford

Bideford

Woolsery

Chittlehamholt

Clyst St Mary

Sidmouth

EXETER

Chagford

Doddiscombsleigh

Topsham

Lydford

Moretonhampstead

Exmouth

Lewdown

North Bovey

Milton Abbot

Two Bridges

Dartmoor National Park

Shaldon

Gulworthy

PLYMOUTH

Plympton

Totnes

Stoke Gabriel

Dartmouth

Kingsbridge

Salcombe

Restaurants listed in the guide correspond to the numbers plotted on the map.

All locations are approximate

NAVAS
PREMIUM BOTANICAL MIXERS
Illuminate your spirit
navasdrinks.com
Blended with Cornish spring water | Partnered with the Eden Project

33 Barbican Kitchen

Modern dining in a historic setting

Brothers Chris and James Tanner celebrate 25 years of cooking in Plymouth this year – 17 of which have been spent at Barbican Kitchen.

Situated inside a historic building that's also home to the Plymouth Gin Distillery (and where the Pilgrim Fathers spent their last night before setting sail on the Mayflower), the restaurant's location makes for an inspiring experience even before you've sampled the food. The ancient stone of the venue is complemented by contemporary styling; the result is a successful marriage of old and new.

A relaxed vibe sets up expectations for a smart casual menu, and the team deliver in style. Dishes are built around locally sourced ingredients such as fish landed by Looe dayboats and meat from Philip Warren Butchers in Launceston. This fine fare is crafted into creations such as Brixham crab salad with grapefruit and avocado, and seared turbot with asparagus, artichokes, pea purée and pancetta. Puds include a delice of chocolate with hazelnut diplomat and milk sorbet.

Committed carnivores will revel in the fruits of Barbican Kitchen's charcoal grill, where West Country moorland beef, dry-aged for succulence, is seared over hot coals for flavour. Just choose a sauce and a starch, such as skinny fries or buttery mash, to accompany.

Plant-based visitors will be pleased by the superb selection of veg-centric dishes, all crafted using hyper-fresh ingredients from the surrounding Devon countryside.

Chef Martyn Compton | **3-course dinner from** £26 | **Seats** 100

barbicankitchen.com | 60 Southside Street, Plymouth Gin Distillery, Plymouth, Devon, PL1 2LQ | 01752 604448

Best Trencherman's Hotel

Boringdon Hall Hotel

TRENCHERMAN'S
AWARDS
2023

**Best
Hotel**

CHURCHILL

'This award recognises the hard work
each member of the team has delivered'

Mathieu Ouvrard, hotel manager

Mathieu Ouvrard of Boringdon Hall Hotel with Lola Grogan of The Eco Laundry (award sponsor)
and Scott Paton (head chef, Àclèaf at Boringdon Hall Hotel)

34 Àclèaf

Michelin-starred dining in Devon

Anyone who has had the pleasure of eating Scott Paton's food in recent years knew it was only a matter of time before the ambitious chef earned a Michelin star for his immaculate creations. The moment finally arrived in early 2023, when Àclèaf was awarded the prestigious accolade.

The intimate restaurant, set inside Grade II-listed Boringdon Hall (which featured in the Domesday Book) near Plymouth, hones in on hyper-seasonal produce. Each dish is carefully planned, beautifully executed and precisely plated by Scott and his dedicated kitchen team.

Scott says: *'Dining at Àclèaf is interactive — a menu with twists and turns along the way.'* The focus is fully on ingredients and the chef expends serious energy, including foraging, to source the best produce for his novel dining experiences.

Hero ingredients on the four-course evening menu include Devon crab, Dartmoor lamb and Highland wagyu, and there are separate menus catering to vegetarian and vegan diners. Scott's nose for palate-pleasing pairings is showcased in an English-led wine flight which takes the dining experience to yet another level.

Trencherman's tip

Book one of the boutique bedrooms and soak in the state-of-the-art Gaia Spa before dinner.

Chef Scott Paton | **4-course dinner from** £120 | **Seats** 40
Bedrooms 55 | **Room rate from** £200 | **EV charging**

acleaf.co.uk | Boringdon Hall Hotel, Boringdon Hill, Plymouth, Devon, PL7 4DP | 01752 344455

35 Twenty-Seven by Jamie Rogers

Culinary wizardry in Kingsbridge

Colours bounce off the plate and flavours pop, delight and ignite curiosity at this Michelin-recommended and two-time Trencherman's Award-winning restaurant (Best Newcomer in 2020 *and* Award for Creativity and Innovation in 2021).

MasterChef: The Professionals semi-finalist Jamie Rogers is the ball of energy who crafts inventive and intriguing dishes from produce sourced within 25 miles of his Kingsbridge restaurant.

Hero ingredients are transformed into creations such as Dartmouth crab mille feuille with cucumber, lime and caviar, and Salcombe Meat Company roasted rack of lamb and slow-cooked shoulder with apricot, courgette and basil.

Guests can dine à la carte for lunch or dinner, but it's worth splashing out to experience

Jamie's culinary wizardry via the six-course tasting menu and complementing wine flight. Plant-based diners are also catered for with tasting menus tailored to vegan and vegetarian diets.

Trencherman's tip

Bookend a meal in style by sipping a pre-dinner cocktail in the elegant downstairs bar before heading upstairs to the intimate loft-like dining room. Then, round off the evening with a zingy apple tarte tatin for two, incorporating cider caramel, Devon Blue and apple cider sorbet.

Chef Jamie Rogers | **3-course dinner from** £65 | **Seats** 40

27devon.co.uk | 9 Mill Street, Kingsbridge, Devon, TQ7 1ED | 01548 288847

Best Newcomer

Andria

'I'm humbled. We've never won anything like this before'

Luca Berardino, chef-owner

Left to right: Lewis Donohoe, Dan Cooper and Luca Berardino of Andria
with *Trencherman's Guide* editor Abi Manning

36 Andria

Buzzy bistro with European flair

The past year has been big for this Dartmouth dining destination. Not only did it receive a mention in the *Michelin Guide*, but it also cemented its status among the South West's hospitality elite by scooping the coveted Best Newcomer prize at the Trencherman's Awards.

The restaurant's success is testament to the determination of chef-owner Luca Berardino and his team who push boundaries and offer a distinctive dining experience.

Named after the Puglian town of Luca's ancestors, Andria is where the talented chef turns his memories and food experiences into unconventional tasting menus and a daily line-up of carefully crafted small plates. Presentation is clean, simple and designed to let bold flavours shine.

Building on his achievements and the restaurant's resulting popularity, Luca has introduced a chef's-table experience above the restaurant, where eight guests are wined and dined in an open kitchen. The immersive supper is all about connection, so book a seat (not a table) to enjoy a menu flush with foraged finds from coast and countryside in the company of other discerning diners.

For something more casual, the lunchtime set menu is excellent value (£35 for four courses, plus canapés and bread) and features the likes of roasted scallop with langoustine bisque and carrot.

Fabulous food is complemented by a lively playlist, relaxed atmosphere and great wines which include an impressive selection by the glass.

Chef Luca Berardino | **3-course dinner from** £40 | **Seats** 32

andriadartmouth.com | 5 Lower Street, Dartmouth, Devon, TQ6 9AJ | 01803 833222

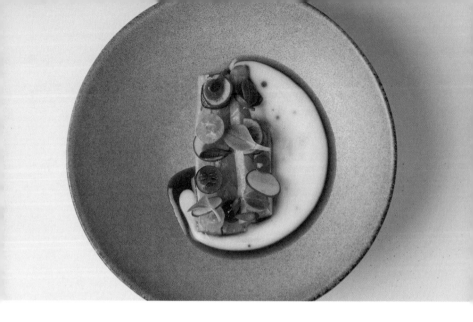

37 The Angel – Taste of Devon

Innovative ideas and intricate plating

MasterChef: The Professionals **finalist Elly Wentworth continues to fly the flag for female chefs from her celebrated Dartmouth restaurant. Joyce Molyneux, the first woman to receive a Michelin star, ran The Angel for 25 years and this spectacular setting is enjoying an exciting era under Elly's tenure.**

The restaurant is a great example of relaxed-yet-refined dining. The team take as much care over guests' comfort as they do in the sourcing, cooking and presentation of delicacies such as roast diver scallops and Devon Red venison.

From the likes of dayboat turbot with broad beans, tarragon and truffle butter to Creedy Carver duck with pickled walnuts, salt-baked kohlrabi and duck jus, every minute detail is fashioned with artistry and an eye for presentation.

The puddings are equally intricate and include delights such as an indulgent "chocolate bar" with layers of lime caramel and pistachio.

Seats by the large picture windows offer views over the harbour, so arrive early and explore the impressive drinks menu (which includes a superb wine list and notable local additions) while watching boats bobbing on the River Dart.

Trencherman's tip

Wine lover? Browse the list online before you visit. Particularly unusual bottles need to be ordered 48 hours in advance.

Chef Elly Wentworth | **3-course dinner from** £80 | **Seats** 26

theangeldartmouth.co.uk | 2 South Embankment, Dartmouth, Devon, TQ6 9BH | 01803 833488

38 Lewtrenchard Manor

A slice of historic grandeur

A visit to this family-run Jacobean manor house is rather like stepping back in time. With wood panelling, stucco ceilings, ancestral portraits and crackling logs lighting up huge elegant fireplaces, Lewtrenchard Manor is a delicious place to dine and stay.

Hidden away in rural Devon, the house is steeped in history and was even mentioned in the Domesday Book. In 1626 it was bought by Henry Gould and remained in the family for generations (eyeball the Gould clan over dinner – their portraits hang in the dining room). Then, in the 19th century, Reverend Sabine Baring-Gould – who penned *Onward Christian Soldiers* – inherited the property and transformed it into the house it is today.

However good Baring-Gould's taste in architecture, it's odds on he didn't have a kitchen crew who could create the kind of beautiful dishes that modern-day visitors experience.

Using fabulously fresh ingredients, including many plucked from the kitchen garden, the team craft à la carte and tasting menus for guests to enjoy in the panelled dining rooms. Dishes include beef tartare with brick pastry, hazelnut, truffle egg-yolk puree and onion, and poached chicken with haricot beans, pancetta, café au lait sauce and truffle powder.

Trencherman's tip

Book the Purple Carrot private chef's table experience with flat-screen views of the kitchen action.

3-course dinner from £65 | Seats 35 | Bedrooms 13 | Room rate from £180

lewtrenchard.co.uk | Lewdown, Okehampton, Devon, EX20 4PN | 01566 783222

39 Hotel Endsleigh

Sophisticated elegance in Devon countryside

Sister to Hotel Tresanton in St Mawes and The Star in Alfriston (East Sussex), Hotel Endsleigh is the Devon contingent of the Polizzi family's trio of gorgeous hotels.

Located on the fringe of Dartmoor, the Grade I-listed former residence of the Duke of Bedford enjoys sweeping views across the Tamar Valley. The scenes from the restaurant and lounge windows are particularly lovely – especially with a glass of Devon's Sharpham wine to hand.

Head chef Thomas Ewings is the man to tempt diners' attention away from the rolling countryside. Smart dishes do justice to luscious local ingredients: try smoked Lydford Estate venison with Pedro Ximénez, hazelnut, cocoa, tomato and cranberry dressing with horseradish, or butter-poached lobster with heritage tomato, globe artichoke, fennel, basil gnocchi, and orange and ginger dressing.

The wood-panelled dining room, complete with roaring fire and original features, makes a fitting backdrop to such splendid feasting. Afterwards, take a stroll in the beautiful grounds, designed by 18th-century English landscape gardener Humphry Repton. Today's horticulturists have been busy uncovering new paths for guests to explore. Keep your eyes peeled for a magical house covered floor-to-ceiling with shells.

Trencherman's tip

Find peaceful repose in this quiet rural setting with an overnight stay in one of the charming bedrooms or spacious Stable Suites, followed by a country-house breakfast the next morning.

Chef Thomas Ewings | **3-course dinner from** £67.50 | **Seats** 40
Bedrooms 19 | **Room rate from** £240 | **EV charging**

thepolizzicollection.com | Milton Abbot, Tavistock, Devon, PL19 0PQ | 01822 870000

40 The Horn of Plenty

Rolling hills and rural charm

Straddling the border between Devon and Cornwall, this secluded country house hotel enjoys sweeping views across the Tamar Valley and is surrounded by five acres of verdant gardens to explore.

Under new ownership since May 2022 and with fresh talent in the kitchen, plans are underway to refresh the hotel while still retaining the rural charm and exceptional dining it's renowned for.

The team of chefs craft seasonally focused menus that capitalise on the South West's bounty of produce from land and sea. Paignton crab, Brixham john dory and Dartmoor venison are just a few of the ingredients that take starring roles on the line-up.

Work is also in progress to reintroduce the hotel's kitchen garden, which will provide a steady supply of seasonal fruit, veg and herbs.

The restaurant takes bookings for lunch, afternoon tea and dinner, but for the full country-house experience book one of the elegant guestrooms and wake up to the sound of birdsong and a hearty home-cooked breakfast.

Trencherman's tip

The Horn of Plenty is a five-minute drive from the pretty market town of Tavistock. Head to its Pannier Market to stock up on artisan produce and browse locally made arts and crafts.

3-course dinner from £69 | Seats 40 | Bedrooms 16 | Room rate from £145 | EV charging

thehornofplenty.co.uk | Gulworthy, Tavistock, Devon, PL19 8JD | 01822 832528

41 Two Bridges Hotel

Dartmoor's destination dining spot

Whether you're looking for a luxurious base from which to explore the moor or a cosy bolthole with roaring fires and superb dining, this hotel and restaurant amid the wilds of Dartmoor offers a guaranteed great escape.

The classic interiors at Two Bridges Hotel are perfect in this moorland environment. Ornate fireplaces, grand old clocks and paintings, polished brass and copper, and a well-stocked bar are precisely what you'd hope to discover after a day tramping over the tussocky hills. Even in bleak midwinter, the attractive hotel is an oasis of hospitality.

Within this characterful setting, talented executive chef Mike Palmer has built a fanbase of foodies who visit the restaurant to delight in globally inspired dishes crafted from local produce. Curations such as

monkfish pakora with mint yogurt, onion bhaji and king prawn masala rub shoulders with Dartmoor lamb with gentleman's relish, potato dauphinoise and pancetta.

Fine wines complement the cooking, and the hotel often hosts wine-pairing dinners. The Two Bridges Devon cream tea is equally noteworthy and best devoured in the gardens after an exhilarating Dartmoor stomp.

Trencherman's tip

Stay over in one of the comfortable bedrooms, complete with four-poster bed and antique furniture.

Chef Mike Palmer | **3-course dinner from** £54 | **Seats** 60 | **Bedrooms** 32 | **Room rate from** £124

twobridges.co.uk | Dartmoor National Park, Devon, PL20 6SW | 01822 892300

42 Bovey Castle

Historic opulence on Dartmoor

From the sweeping driveway leading to the neo-Elizabethan manor house to the warm welcome from the porter, a visit to Bovey Castle always starts in style.

The impressive venue is set within 275 acres of lush countryside on the edge of Dartmoor, and guests can indulge in an array of traditional English country pursuits, from clay pigeon shooting and off-road driving experiences to fly fishing and falconry. There's also an 18-hole championship golf course for those wishing to tee off.

After an action-packed day of activities or a more leisurely stint of pampering in the Elan Spa, guests can choose to dine in one of two restaurants. Smith's Brasserie offers Mediterranean-inspired pizza, pasta and small plates in a relaxed and informal setting, while the three-AA-rosette Great Western Grill creates more traditional experiences. The latter has recently reopened following a major refurb and now includes a Champagne and Oyster Bar.

Head chef Mark Budd puts a modern spin on classic dishes such as red-wine braised oxtail cottage pie with horseradish mash, and poached native lobster and truffle macaroni cheese with confit tomato. Both restaurants make the most of the estate's abundant produce, including seasonal vegetables and locally reared beef and game.

Trencherman's tip

Book in for afternoon tea in the Great Western Grill, with options for gluten-free, vegetarian and vegan diets.

Chef Mark Budd | **3-course dinner from** £55 | **Seats** 70
Bedrooms 60, plus 22 lodges | **Room rate from** £239 | **EV charging**
boveycastle.com | North Bovey, Devon, TQ13 8RE | 01647 445000

43 The NoBody Inn

Whisky galore in the countryside

This charming 17th-century inn in the Devon village of Doddiscombsleigh has long enjoyed a solid reputation for excellent wining and dining.

Off the beaten track in countryside not far from Exeter, it's so tucked away you'd never just stumble across it. But those in the know visit for the lovely cooking and incredible drinks collection: 240 whiskies and 30 wines by the glass, plus an impressive cellar of bottles from across the globe.

It's a dining spot for all seasons, and in summer foodies make a beeline for the garden. However, The NoBody Inn is undoubtedly at its most atmospheric in the depths of winter when low ceilings, blackened beams and period features combine with the crackle of smouldering logs in the grate and the soft glow of candlelight.

Even if wine and whisky aren't your bag, you'll undoubtedly find a spirit to seduce you – the orange notes of the house gin are a good place to start – as well as a sterling collection of ales and beers.

The pleasures extend way beyond those of the liquid variety: the crowd-pleasing cooking (crafted from a wealth of locally produced ingredients) deftly walks the line between smart and hearty. Ingredients such as local venison and fish from the Devon coast are treated with cheerful reverence.

Trencherman's tip

Attractive guestrooms make The NoBody Inn a great spot for a gourmet getaway, solving the 'who'll be designated driver?' argument.

3-course dinner from £35 | Seats 45 | Bedrooms 5 | Room rate from £105

nobodyinn.co.uk | Doddiscombsleigh, Exeter, Devon, EX6 7PS | 01647 252394

44 The Salutation Inn

Refined Topsham dining

Those seeking a culinary interlude on their way from London to Cornwall, or somewhere luxurious to sleep on the outskirts of Exeter, should book a dine-and-stay experience at this charming restaurant with rooms in the heart of Topsham.

The historic port town on the winding River Exe – located just off the M5 yet close to countryside – is a hub of indie shops, restaurants and waterside pubs.

The Salutation Inn has been at its heart since 1720 and has a long history of serving patrons as a pub. However, when Tom and Amelia Williams-Hawkes took over in 2012, they transformed it into a refined dining destination.

Over the past decade, the couple have garnered a fantastic reputation for serving some of the best food in the area. The à la carte and tasting menus have a piscatorial leaning (Tom's dad was a salmon fisherman for 30 years) but also showcase some of the region's finest meat and veg producers. Dishes such as ponzu-glazed crab mousse served with shellfish mayo and sesame seaweed are composed creatively and presented beautifully by head chef Luke Heaver.

Trencherman's tip

Stopping off on your way to self-catered accommodation or en route home? Pick up fresh local seafood from the in-house wet fish deli, Salt.

Chef Luke Heaver | **3-course dinner from** £35 | **Seats** 40 | **Bedrooms** 6 | **Room rate from** £100

salutationtopsham.co.uk | 68 Fore Street, Topsham, Devon, EX3 0HL | 01392 873060

45 The Galley Restaurant

Seafood with style in Topsham

Fresh-from-the-ocean seafood is the calling card of this buzzy award-winning restaurant, just a stone's throw from the River Exe.

Located in a charmingly crooked 18th-century townhouse, The Galley has an intimate bistro vibe that makes it an ideal date-night venue. Reserve a table for two and indulge in a couple or three courses from the fish-forward menu paired with something special from the extensive wine list.

New head chef Jack Harvey honed his craft working in London at various establishments run by Marcus Wareing. Specialising in bold, clean flavours, he regularly updates the line-up depending on the day's catch. Expect to find the likes of crab tartlet with brown and white crab, avocado, fennel, grapefruit and coriander to start, followed by mains

such as roasted monkfish tail with tomato, black olive, mussels and romesco sauce. The carefully curated menu always includes quality meat and vegetarian options too.

This year has seen The Galley adorned with an array of accolades. A Michelin plate was swiftly followed by a Bib Gourmand, and the restaurant has gained entry into *Hardens*.

Trencherman's tip

Leave room for a rather epic cheeseboard, featuring South West favourites like Ticklemore (crafted with Devon goat's milk) and brie made by the dairy pros at Sharpham in South Devon.

Chef Jack Harvey | **3-course dinner from** £36.50 | **Seats** 48

galleyrestaurant.co.uk | 41 Fore Street, Topsham, Devon, EX3 0HU | 01392 876078

46 Lympstone Manor

Star-quality luxury

Having cemented its status as the epitome of comfort, exclusivity and luxury, Michael Caines' modern take on the country house hotel continues to dazzle.

Lympstone's star status remains steadfast, having been named Best Dining Experience in the UK at the Condé Nast Johansens Awards for Excellence 2023, and retaining its five AA rosettes and Michelin star this year.

Chef-owner Michael and his kitchen brigade craft tasting and à la carte menus loaded with local flavours from land and sea. Immaculately plated dishes such as Darts Farm chicken and truffle terrine with braised leeks, truffle mayonnaise, green bean and truffle tartlet with Madeira jelly sit alongside braised Cornish turbot, morels, spring peas and asparagus with a chive and truffle butter sauce. Dine in one

of three exquisite rooms named after views across the estuary: Powderham, Mamhead and Berry Head.

The experience is incomplete without sampling artfully matched wines from the world-class cellar – this year the list includes Lympstone Manor Cuvée, pressed from grapes grown on the 11-acre vineyard.

Beyond spectacular dining, there are numerous other delights to indulge in such as a stay in a beautiful room, suite or one of six shepherd's huts, as well as a game of tennis or a wander in the sculpture garden.

Trencherman's tip

Take a dip in the new outdoor pool with stunning views across the vineyard and over to the Exe Estuary, before a casual bite to eat at the Pool House Restaurant and Bar.

Chef Michael Caines MBE | **3-course dinner from** £155 | **Seats** 60
Bedrooms and shepherd's huts 27 | **Room rate from** £395 | **EV charging**

lympstonemanor.co.uk | Courtlands Lane, Exmouth, Devon, EX8 3NZ | 01395 202040

Best Bar List
The Farmers Arms

'Our goal has always been to do something unique while not alienating guests'

Harry Brooks, beverage manager

Left to right: Harry Brooks and Jay Oyarzabel of The Farmers Arms
with Hayley Reynolds of RAW PR (event partner)

47 The Farmers Arms

A new kind of traditional Devon pub

Imagine the dream dining pub: a creative chef crafts sublime dishes; its own farm supplies the homegrown, reared and foraged produce; an innovative drinks line-up utilises handcrafted cordials and own-infused spirits, and it's all complemented by accommodation that mixes vintage glamour with modern luxury.

A visit to The Farmers Arms (part of The Collective at Woolsery, a curation of village enterprises from tech entrepreneurs Michael and Xochi Birch) combines all of the above, and is going from strength to strength as the team further develop the farm and gardens that stock the pub kitchen with hyper-seasonal produce.

Dine in any of the three beautifully rustic dining rooms, or bag a table in the garden courtyard to feast alfresco on head chef Ian Webber's reinterpretations of British classics. The own-reared lamb, pork and hogget are notable highlights on a menu that's elevated further by daily picked veg, fruit and herbs.

On Sundays, plump for a family-style lunch (meat or veggie) to gorge on a waistband-stretching smorgasbord of roast favourites such as Exmoor beef brisket, indulgent cauliflower cheese and proper yorkshire puddings.

Trencherman's tip

Make a weekend of it by booking one of the gorgeous suites or rooms above the village shop (also part of The Collective at Woolsery) or push the boat out with a few nights in one of the three ultra-luxe cottages.

Chef Ian Webber | **3-course dinner from** £35 | **Seats** 50 | **Bedrooms** 7 | **Room rate from** £275

woolsery.com | Woolsery, Devon, EX39 5QS | 01237 439328

48 Number Eight

Global fusion in north Devon

A slew of accolades (including Best Restaurant at the Trencherman's Awards 2021 and Best Restaurant in the Food Reader Awards 2020) has cemented Number Eight's reputation as one of the region's most exciting places to dine.

As stalwarts of the hospitality scene in Cornwall, Joshua Jones and Chloe Wilks had plenty of industry experience to draw on when they crossed the border to launch their own restaurant in north Devon five years ago.

Going it alone was bold, but it paid off. Joshua's continuously evolving tasting menus have developed a fanbase of foodies who travel from across the region to sample them.

The kitchen is a solo operation, with Joshua carefully sourcing top-notch produce for his global fusion dishes which include crispy Korean pig's cheek and Indian-style Cornish hake, as well as Appledore scallops caught from the nearby village and served with rhubarb, Champagne and artichoke. Chloe, meanwhile, is the friendly face out front who looks after diners with warmth, calm and efficiency.

In summer 2022, the restaurant moved from its unassuming location down a Bideford side street to a freshly renovated quayside venue in the town.

Trencherman's tip

There's no online booking system here – Chloe prefers to deal with each customer on a personal level via an old-school phone call or email.

Chef Joshua Jones | **Tasting menu from** £85 | **Seats** 22

numbereightrestaurant.com | 49 Torrington Street, Bideford, Devon, EX39 4DP | 01237 237589

49 The Fig Tree @ 36

Plymouth's little slice of Paris

The Fig Tree picked up the Best Restaurant gong at the Food Drink Devon Awards 2022, testament to the neighbourhood bistro's sterling reputation with locals and visitors alike.

Its Trust the Chef menu (which offers three courses for £29 at lunch and £39 at dinner) has proved so popular that owners Ryan and Tanya Marsland have extended its availability to every day the restaurant is open.

Head chef Ryan's dishes are a celebration of Devon's fruitful land and sea, with hero ingredients like just-landed River Exe mussels, Plymouth monkfish and Copplestone chicken sourced from the region's top producers.

The line-up changes daily, but guests will discover a French leaning in dishes such as fish stew of gurnard, skate, mussels, fennel and samphire, served with aioli and warm bread.

If the forecast is favourable, book one of the tables under the fig tree in the garden and kick off an alfresco supper with cocktails, plump olives and homemade bread. The restaurant is tucked away on a residential street a short walk from Royal William Yard – perfect for a post-lunch stroll along the harbour.

Trencherman's tip

Visit in the daytime to pick up takeaway treats at the deli. Highlights include the hot pork-belly sandwich and Fowey mussels with warm bread and aioli.

Chef Ryan Marsland | **3-course dinner from** £39 | **Seats** 40

thefigtreeat36.co.uk | 36 Admiralty Street, Plymouth, Devon, PL1 3RU | 01752 253247

50 Salumi Bar & Eatery

Flexible dining for all appetites

Salumi has established itself as a go-to eatery for many Plymouth residents thanks to its flexible dining approach and uber-friendly service. Whether it's a family Sunday lunch, a date-night dinner, or cocktails and a sharing board with friends, all bases are covered.

Inside, bright turquoise-painted tables, chairs and fittings contrast with oak beams and exposed brick walls to create a rustic vibe. Seating is split across multiple levels and there's a large outdoor courtyard area with wooden benches and a fire kitchen, where many of the dishes are prepared.

Chefs Dave Jenkins and Jake Hardington have created menus to suit any whim, be it full-blown feasting or nibbles over drinks. Lunchtime bagels – topped with the likes of Welsh rarebit, spiced tomato and red pepper chutney, sauerkraut and crispy onion – delight casual diners, while those after something more formal will find it in the prix fixe lunch and evening à la carte menus.

The food is modern British but with Asian influences aplenty. Take the Sunday lunch menu, which features traditional roasts alongside a smattering of surprises such as barbecue king-oyster-mushroom bao buns, and yaki udon with seaweed, shimeji mushroom and bok choy.

Trencherman's tip

Sunday roasts are served from 11am till 8pm but are extremely popular, so booking is advised.

Chefs Dave Jenkins and Jake Hardington | **3-course dinner from** £30 | **Seats** 50

eatsalumi.co.uk | 18 Millbay Road, Plymouth, Devon, PL1 3LH | 01752 267538

51 Fletcher's Restaurant

Intimate and authentic

A glowing fairy-light-filled entrance and relaxed ambience create an inviting welcome for visitors to this popular Plymouth restaurant.

With high-street chains ubiquitous across UK city centres, it can be a challenge finding distinguished independents that deliver on both quality and atmosphere. Thankfully, family-run Fletcher's hits the mark, offering refined dining in a relaxed yet intimate setting.

Whether diners are celebrating a special occasion or seeking a showstopping pre-theatre feed, chef-patron Fletcher Andrews' elegant dishes won't fail to impress.

For the full Fletcher's experience, opt for the seven-course tasting menu to sample the chef's vibrant flavours. Quail breast is served with quail farce, sweetcorn puree, charred corn with a black garlic puree and quail sauce, while pan-fried halibut is elevated with British asparagus, wild garlic garganelli and pickled cucumber.

Desserts such as chamomile mousse and yuzu ganache served with malt, honey and white chocolate ice cream provide a beautiful finishing note, the culinary symphony rounded off by exquisitely presented petits fours.

Trencherman's tip

Heading to Theatre Royal Plymouth after your meal? Reserve your pre-show feast at nearby Fletcher's well in advance as tables get booked up fast.

Chef Fletcher Andrews | **3-course dinner from** £45 | **Seats** 45

fletchersrestaurant.co.uk | 27 Princess Street, Plymouth, Devon, PL1 2EX | 01752 201523

52 The Jetty at Salcombe Harbour Hotel

Spectacular views and sumptuous seafood

There are few better views of Salcombe Estuary than those from The Jetty Restaurant at Salcombe Harbour Hotel. As the sun slips below the horizon, the restaurant's terrace is a fabulous spot for drinking in the vista with a cocktail to hand.

The panorama isn't The Jetty's only draw, however. Fresh fish and signature dishes from head chef Jamie Gulliford ensure the restaurant is permanently buzzing. House favourites include the surf-and-turf platter and plump hake fillet topped with a crab and herb crust.

Longstanding relationships with local fishermen ensure the latest catch is always on offer, yet the daily menu is not exclusively pescatarian. The twice-baked cheese soufflé and the succulent lamb grazed on south Devon pasture are just as popular.

The restaurant offers an all-day menu with the same beguiling options running from lunch to dinner, and is open to residents and non-residents alike.

Those wishing to stay the night will find many of the spacious rooms have waterfront views and all guests gain access to the subterranean spa. Each room comes with complementary decanters of gin and sherry, so guests can raise a toast to a delicious south coast staycation.

Trencherman's tip

Cocktails and an order of cockle popcorn are the way to kick off an evening's feasting – Jetty style.

Chef Jamie Gulliford | **3-course dinner from** £38 | **Seats** 96
Bedrooms 50 | **Room rate from** £220 | **EV charging**
harbourhotels.co.uk/salcombe | Cliff Road, Salcombe, Devon, TQ8 8JH | 01548 844444

53 Circa

Wine and dine experience

Those looking for a one-of-a-kind venue will be hard pressed to find anything quite like Circa. Located in a former milking parlour on the grounds of an award-winning winery, it's a special place for feasting on fodder sourced from the surrounding rolling hills of the Dart Valley.

With some of the best produce in the UK grown and reared in the fields that border the vineyard, chef-founder Rob Weeks gets first pick of the freshest veg and grass-fed meat, while fish and shellfish is landed daily at nearby Brixham. The ambitious chef favours organic ingredients wherever possible, and lets what's available each morning guide his constantly changing menus.

Lunch and dinner service is a sharing-style set-up, with two or three dishes recommended per person. Diners can expect to tuck into small plates such as cep dumplings with charred vegetables, fava beans, shiitake and coffee kombucha, and beef shin and Pinot Noir croquettes served with black garlic and celeriac.

The restaurant's location on the Sandridge Barton estate means wine is very much part of the Circa experience. The front-of-house team can recommend an excellent match to the menu selections, although it would be remiss not to kick off proceedings with a glass of Sharpham's Classic Cuvée 2020.

Trencherman's tip

Stay overnight at the vineyard by booking one of the three on-site self-catering holiday cottages.

Chef Rob Weeks | **3-course dinner from** £40 | **Seats** 75

circadevon.co.uk | Lower Well Farm, Sandridge Barton, Stoke Gabriel, Devon, TQ9 6RL | 01803 732203

54 Gather

Authentic farm-to-table dining

Any chef worth their salt knows where their produce comes from, yet the zealous team at this Totnes restaurant go the extra mile by personally foraging many of the ingredients on the menu.

For chefs Harrison Brockington and Oli Rosier, showcasing the unique flavours of Devon's fields, shoreline, rivers and hedgerows is the underlying principle of everything they do. This deep connection with their environment is expressed in full and half tasting menus, which are tweaked daily and revised monthly to reflect what's fresh and in season.

Along with their foraged finds, the pair choose local suppliers whose ethos aligns with the restaurant's climate-conscious principles. Meat reared in the South Hams comes courtesy of Christopher McCabe Butchers, while seasonal and organic veg is supplied by a smallholding a few miles away.

Constant refinement and unshackled creativity result in dynamic and exciting dishes that appeal to the culinarily curious. Treacle tart, for example, is served with blue cheese and gooseberries, while hedgerow tortellini is elevated with foraged herbs.

The front-of-house staff are well versed on the day's menu and their informed-yet-friendly service style creates a warm and welcoming ambience. Both tasting options have an accompanying wine flight, but if you'd rather go off-menu the team are always happy to suggest an alternative pairing.

Trencherman's tip

Check Gather's website for upcoming events, including collaborations with local producers and foraged tasting suppers.

Chef Harrison Brockington | **3-course dinner from** £30 | **Seats** 25

gathertotnes.com | 50 Fore Street, Totnes, Devon, TQ9 5RP | 01803 866666

55 The Dartmoor Inn at Lydford

Sophisticated Dartmoor dining

There are countless country inns where you can rock up at the bar in your wellies following a moorland yomp. But for those seeking something smarter than post-hike pub grub, The Dartmoor Inn strikes the balance between cosy bar and smart restaurant – and has made a name for itself among savvy foodies seeking contemporary Dartmoor dining.

Since taking over the pub in 2019, chef Jay Barker-Jones and wife Tess (front of house) have been racking up the awards. The pub has recently won Silver at both the South West Tourism Awards and Devon Tourism Awards, and was a finalist for Front of House Team at the Trencherman's Awards 2023.

In the kitchen, Jay focuses on crafting refined fare which is served in a thoroughly unstuffy setting. His ever-developing menus reflect what's in season and produced locally. For a taste of Dartmoor, opt for starters like tender wood pigeon accompanied by jerusalem artichoke, hazelnut, mushroom and blackberries, followed by superstar mains like glazed pork belly with sage and onion sausage roll, spring vegetables, mustard emulsion and apple.

The culinary offering also includes a cracking seafood selection: dishes such as Atlantic cod with cauliflower, coconut, curry broth and coriander are manna for fish fans.

Trencherman's tip

The drinks experience is as carefully crafted as the food. The list has recently been expanded to include more cocktails, wines by the glass and non-alcoholic options, while speciality coffee beans roasted down the road at Okehampton's No.1 Coffee make for quality post-dinner caffeination.

Chef Jay Barker-Jones | **3-course dinner from** £39 | **Seats** 60 | **Bedrooms** 3 | **Room rate from** £109

dartmoorinn.com | Moorside, Lydford, Okehampton, Devon, EX20 4AY | 01822 820221

56 Mill End Hotel and Restaurant

Decadent feasting on Dartmoor

This converted 15th-century flour mill, perched on the banks of the River Teign, is an idyllic spot for lunch, afternoon tea or a candlelit dinner after a day on Dartmoor.

Whether you plump for the daytime Lounge and Lawn menu or visit for the à la carte line-up, relish the fact that almost every element on your plate has been crafted in-house by head chef William Broom and his kitchen crew. This includes the bread, cakes, sauces and even the bottled water, which is tapped on-site from a deep moorland source before going through a seven-stage filtration and purification process.

Dinner is a decadent affair featuring locally landed seafood, South West cheeses, meat from nearby farms and moorland game, which are fashioned into thoughtful dishes plated with flair. Pig's head terrine with celeriac remoulade, cornichons, pickled walnut and date ketchup; Creedy Carver duck with glazed faggot, celeriac, clapshot, creamed cabbage and braised lentils; and warm dark chocolate bon bon with coffee ice cream and Dartmoor Whisky cream are a taste of some of the dishes on offer.

In the summer months, bag a table in the lush garden to munch on more casual plates such as a ploughman's lunch or a Mill FLT (fish finger, lettuce and tomato) sandwich.

Trencherman's tip

Mill End has a number of bespoke rooms and suites especially for guests and their canine companions. Pampered pooches will be waited on hand and paw throughout their stay with welcome packs, breakfast sausages and dining areas in all key parts of the hotel.

Chef William Broom | **3-course dinner from** £45 | **Seats** 43
Bedrooms 21 | **Room rate from** £150 | **EV charging**

millendhotel.com | Chagford, Newton Abbot, Devon, TQ13 8JN | 01647 432282

57 The Horse

Moreish pizzas on the moor

Dartmoor pubs may tend to serve traditional fodder, but this gem in the market town of Moretonhampstead offers a far more unusual experience than the standard roast with all the trimmings.

Head to the family-run pub for Mediterranean-inspired cooking in a classic pub setting. Chef-owner Nigel Hoyle dishes up a menu that majors on pizzas, but don't let this put you off as these are far from the ordinary takeaway variety.

Thin-crust, twice-risen focaccia dough is piled with locally sourced and Italian-imported artisan ingredients. Crowd-pleasing combos include the Vesuvio ('nduja sausage, chorizo, fresh onions, confit potatoes, buffalo mozzarella and oregano) and The Eastern (spiced lamb, peppers, cumin-roasted onions, harissa and tahini).

Away from the pizza oven, there's a regularly rotating selection of seasonal specialities. Try home-cured bresaola (Dartmoor beef topside cured for two weeks in red wine) served with Indian achar pickle and goat's cheese, or the vegan super salad featuring cumin-roasted onions, cauliflower, broccoli and spiced dukkah with a zingy lime dressing and vegan yogurt.

It's a great spot to visit with a crowd so you can order a range of antipasti and pizzas. What you can't eat can be taken home in a takeaway container.

Trencherman's tip

G&T fans can select their spirit of choice from the lengthy list of uber-local Papillon Gins, which are distilled just next door.

Chef Nigel Hoyle | **3-course dinner from £22** | **Seats** 60

thehorsedartmoor.co.uk | 7 George Street, Moretonhampstead, Devon, TQ13 8PG | 01647 440242

58 ODE – true food

Sustainable suppers in Shaldon

Ness Cove in Shaldon is famous for its smuggler's tunnel and picturesque beach, but epicureans in the area know it best for its day-to-night dining concept: ODE – true food.

A buzzy, casual cafe by day, award-winning ODE transforms into a smart supper destination by night. Chef-proprietor Tim Bouget trained under Michel Roux at The Waterside Inn at Bray and brings creative flair to dishes that draw the best from Devon's abundant larder.

Haldon fallow deer burger, pulled organic pork with south Devon chipotle, and native lobster bisque are a few of the dishes that appear on a line-up that changes weekly to reflect what's in season. Having worked overseas for many years, Tim also likes to pepper his menus with dishes inspired by his travels in North Africa and Asia.

Sustainability is central to the ODE ethos (it won a Cateys Sustainable Business Award in 2014), and the theme runs through everything from the building's structure (solar panels, lambswool insulation and a living sedum roof) to the reclaimed wood furniture. In the open-plan kitchen, the chefs use 100 per cent renewable energy to craft dishes made with local ingredients selected for their low food miles.

Trencherman's tip

In the summer, wood-fired sourdough pizzas are served from a vintage horsebox on the terrace.

Chef Tim Bouget | **3-course dinner from** £37 | **Seats** 20 | **EV charging**
odetruefood.com | Ness Cove, Ness Drive, Shaldon, Devon, TQ14 0HP | 01626 873427

59 Mickeys Beach

Caines' laid-back beachside joint

The most relaxed member of the Michael Caines Collection, Mickeys Beach may be less formal in style and service than its stablemates (which include Michelin-starred Lympstone Manor just up the road) but it's no less inviting.

Caines dreamed of creating a venue that would encapsulate the social joy of informal seaside dining, whether that's enjoying fabulous food or simply a cocktail and nibbles. The result is this laid-back, family-friendly restaurant and bar, part of Exmouth's Sideshore watersports centre.

Downstairs is a large bar area with an informal menu – an ideal spot for light lunches with family and friends (pooches are also welcome). For a romantic meal or celebratory occasion, opt for a table in Mickeys Beach Restaurant upstairs. The atmosphere is equally fun but the ocean views are even more astounding.

This is a place where you can let your hair down, but rest assured there's no compromise on quality. Everything Michael puts his name to is top-notch, from the Mickeys Beach burgers to the Neapolitan-style pizzas (try the Golosona for a rich blend of blue cheese, artichoke, red pepper and spicy salami). Fresh fish is sourced direct from Lyme Bay and expertly cooked over charcoal.

Trencherman's tip

For a very special Sunday lunch, book in for Mickeys Roast on the Coast to get stuck into meltingly tender Devon-reared meats cooked on the spit over coals. Uber-local suppliers include Darts Farm and Lashbrook Farm.

Chef Alex Gibbs | **3-course dinner from** £35 | **Seats** 42 | **EV charging**

mickeysbeach.co.uk | Unit 1, Sideshore, Queen's Drive, Exmouth, Devon, EX8 2GD | 01395 206888

60 Saveur

Euro-inspired cooking in Exmouth

**There's no need to cross the Channel
to experience Parisian bistro vibes
when a seaside excursion to Exmouth
reveals a vraiment délicieux dining
encounter at Saveur.**

Hidden away on a pedestrianised street just
off the main square, this local favourite is
where chef-patron Nigel Wright leads a
kitchen crew whose modern, seasonal dishes
have seen the restaurant retain its two AA
rosettes for six years.

The kitchen continues to develop daily
changing menus that celebrate all things
local and seasonal, with a leaning towards
seafood thanks to the venue's proximity
to the ocean (and Nigel's hotline to the
fishmongers at Brixham Fish Market). A
starter of seared local sesame scallop with
spring onion, ginger soy dressing and crispy
seaweed can be chased by hake with crab
velouté, grilled little gem and watercress

potatoes. The catch of the day is available for
diners who want to experience the dayboats'
freshest haul.

For those not piscatorially inclined, the
options are equally delicious; seasonal
examples include local venison with pommes
anna, smoked celeriac puree, roasted beets
and sherry jus.

The service is as relaxed and welcoming
as the decor, making this a charming
find for a casual lunch with friends or an
intimate dinner à deux.

Trencherman's tip

Want to make the most of the restrained
but impressive wine list? Saveur is just a
30-minute train ride from Exeter.

Chef Nigel Wright | **3-course dinner from** £36 | **Seats** 20

saveursrestaurant.com | 9 Tower Street, Exmouth, Devon, EX8 1NT | 01395 269459

61 Winslade Manor Bar & Restaurant

Understated luxury

Nestled amid 86 acres of stunning parkland on the outskirts of Exeter, 19th-century Winslade Manor exudes understated luxury and is an idyllic place for business lunches, group celebrations, or relaxing gourmet getaways.

Whatever the occasion, the lovingly restored manor offers a variety of spaces in which to unwind. Find a quiet corner in the lounge to curl up on a comfy sofa, sip a signature cocktail in the contemporary bar or pull up a pew in the characterful dining room.

The restaurant's reputation is built on refined and exciting food experiences. Award-winning executive chef Matt Mason utilises local ingredients to create dishes that celebrate England's eclectic culinary influences while simultaneously focusing on sustainability and innovation.

Everything is made in-house, and there are menu choices to suit all occasions, from brunch and express lunches to seven-course tasting experiences – all supported by a drinks menu that showcases local beers, classic cocktails and wines from independent vineyards.

On fine days, the terrace is a charming spot for a casual alfresco lunch with family and friends or to entertain business clients in a relaxed atmosphere overlooking lush greenery.

Trencherman's tip

Need a pick-me-up? Try the Winslade Wellbeing Bowl. This variation on bibimbap is a Korean rice bowl with warm sticky rice, edamame beans, pickled shiitake mushrooms, sesame carrots, beansprouts, fried egg, coriander and a choice of chicken, trout, prawns or tofu.

Chef Matt Mason | **3-course dinner from** £35 | **Seats** 40

winslademanor.com | Winslade Park Avenue, Manor Drive, Exeter, Devon, EX5 1FY | 01392 640644

62 The Riviera Hotel and Restaurant

Sidmouth's seaside charm

This imposing establishment on Sidmouth's esplanade offers charming English seaside views and smart two-AA-rosette dining.

Attention to detail is the defining characteristic of chef Patrice Bouffaut's modern British menus. Stay close to home with a roast rack of Devonshire lamb, set on minted couscous and served with ratatouille, red wine shallots and a minted jus. Or opt for steamed paupiette of lemon sole (supplied by a third-generation local fishing family) filled with a salmon mousse and baby spinach, served with couscous, asparagus, tomato compote and a saffron foam.

For those seeking a gourmet getaway, glorious sea views can be enjoyed from many of the tastefully furnished bedrooms. Guests are impeccably well looked after as the hotel is known for its genuine welcome, traditional hospitality and superb service.

The Riviera makes an elegant base from which to explore Sidmouth, a resort described by poet laureate John Betjeman as *'a town caught still in timeless charm'*. Its public gardens, bandstands, putting greens and croquet lawns continue to attract those in search of relaxation and tranquil pleasures, while a lively folk festival takes place in August.

Trencherman's tip

Get into the glamorous spirit of the place by sipping a cocktail in the Regency Bar or linger over a lunch of classic dishes out on the sunny terrace.

Chef Patrice Bouffaut | **3-course dinner from** £50 | **Seats** 80
Bedrooms 26 | **Room rate from** £250

hotelriviera.co.uk | The Esplanade, Sidmouth, Devon, EX10 8AY | 01395 515201

63 The Mole Resort

Family staycation destination

Classic and contemporary combine at this hotel, resort and restaurant in the wilds of north Devon. Formerly Highbullen Hotel, the estate has recently rebranded and relaunched as The Mole Resort, a contemporary destination for family breaks and active escapes.

The Arts and Crafts-era house has been respectfully refurbished and remains the focal point of the estate — book a stay in one of its Manor or Estate rooms to be in the heart of the hotel. The addition of 58 new luxury lodges within the grounds has enabled the resort to embrace larger groups and self-catered stays. Each one has a hot tub and private balcony, and there's even an energy-positive lodge that creates more energy than it uses (the first of its kind in the UK).

Depending on their mood, guests can choose between the Cellar's Bar and Restaurant and the more casual Bistro. Both follow the resort's sustainable ethos of using seasonal local produce, and the team know many of the farmers who supply the kitchen by name.

The Library is a grown-ups-only space to kick back with a cocktail. The bar is stocked with artisan spirits, including The Mole's own tequila, gin and rum, which are distilled in Somerset, plus craft beers such as The Mole IPA.

Trencherman's tip

The Mole is made for active family breaks. Adrenalin-spiking activities include tennis, archery, axe throwing, swimming, golf and bushcraft.

Chef Stephen Walker | **3-course dinner from** £45 | **Seats** 90
Bedrooms 83 | **Room rate from** £137 | **EV charging**
themoleresort.co.uk | Chittlehamholt, Umberleigh, Devon, EX37 9HD | 01769 540561

64 Canvas Restaurant at Broomhill Estate

Art and culinary artistry collide

Broomhill Estate has long been loved for its sculpture gardens and art installations, but it recently relaunched its restaurant with a culinary offering that's as carefully curated as the visual feast surrounding diners.

The new concept, called Canvas, features evolving menus that give a snapshot of the best produce available at any given moment in the season (the first menu celebrated British summertime – think fresh berries and barbecues). Menus sit alongside changing exhibitions, taking guests on a uniquely aesthetic restaurant experience.

The dining format has also been updated with three-course set menu and Signature Palette menu options, which executive chef Elio Debae crafts from exclusively British ingredients – including produce from the estate itself. Expect the likes of ceviche scallops with fermented celeriac,

lemon verbena and estate-grown sprout kimchi, and foraged blackberry sorbet with surplus-Prosecco oxymel and fennel pollen.

Thoughtful drinks pairings are selected to complement the menu, and there's also a new craft cocktail programme. Signature Canvas cocktails riff on classics while using the best of what's available from the surrounding countryside, such as in the Fig Leaf Martini.

For those staying over there are seven boutique bedrooms, each inspired by a cult film. Alternatively, feel at one with nature by parking up your campervan in the woods for a spot of wild camping.

Trencherman's tip

Take your drink to the film lounge to admire authentic props from films like *Fight Club* and *Alien vs. Predator* while you sip.

Chef Elio Debae | **3-course dinner from** £50 | **Seats** 20
Bedrooms 7 | **Room rate from** £180 | **EV charging**

broomhill-estate.com | Broomhill Estate, Muddiford, Barnstaple, Devon, EX31 4EX | 01271 850262

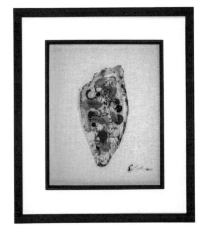

Dorset & Hampshire

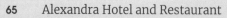
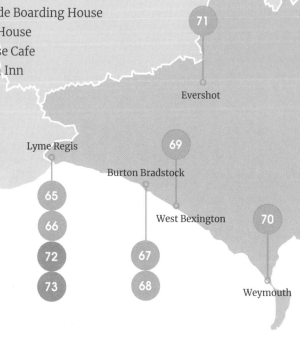

71

Evershot

Lyme Regis

Burton Bradstock

69

West Bexington

70

65

66

72

73

67

68

Weymouth

BOURNEMOUTH

Christchurch

74

75

**Restaurants listed in the guide correspond
to the numbers plotted on the map.**

All locations are approximate

PKF
FRANCIS
CLARK
Shared Ambition

Accounting | Advisory | Audit | Tax

pkf-francisclark.co.uk

65 Alexandra Hotel and Restaurant

Long-standing Lyme Regis favourite

The buzzy seaside town of Lyme Regis hums with activity in the warmer months, but the coastal hideaway of Alexandra Hotel and Restaurant – perched high up in the cliffs – feels a world away from the hubbub.

Its spacious lawns are charming to wander through – glass of fizz in hand – and enjoy a moment of tranquility. The views and mature gardens are complemented by smart interiors designed in eclectic country style, and there's something interesting to catch the eye on every shelf and wall – especially in the maritime-themed sitting room.

However, beyond all these attractions, foodies favour the 18th-century hotel for its contemporary British cooking which can be experienced within its two restaurants. The Ammonite restaurant in the orangery is a vision of floral loveliness, thanks to its elegant decor and views over the attractive gardens (it also has a glassed-over ancient well in the middle of the floor). Or pick the cool blues of the seashell-adorned Alexandra Restaurant for evening feasting; it's especially pretty by the glow of candlelight.

Wherever you dine, expect an elegant menu swimming with freshly caught local fish and shellfish such as lobster and hand-dived scallops.

Trencherman's tip

For a romantic occasion, private dining for two in the Lookout Tower is a special option. And if your significant other says 'yes', you could even return to get hitched in the hotel's old chapel.

Chef Chris Chatfield | **3-course dinner from** £30 | **Seats** 70
Bedrooms 23 | **Room rate from** £180 | **EV charging**

hotelalexandra.co.uk | Pound Street, Lyme Regis, Dorset, DT7 3HZ | 01297 442010

66 Robin Wylde

Micro-seasonal menus

With mentions in the *Michelin Guide*, *The Good Food Guide* and Harden's Top 100 Restaurants, Robin Wylde has garnered national attention for its micro-seasonal and hyper-local exploration of Dorset's coast and countryside.

Each course at the pleasingly intimate restaurant is described to the diner as it's delivered to the table, with seasonal examples including wild garlic and kombucha crème fraîche doughnut; nettle, cod roe and carrot; and flowering quince custard tart and rhubarb.

The team scour the diverse landscape surrounding the Lyme Regis restaurant for wild herbs, fruit and vegetables, which often results in unfamiliar (yet delicious) ingredients making it onto the adventurous menus.

Oenophiles will delight in the beautifully paired wines – usually biodynamic or organic – and there's also an excellent non-alcoholic drinks flight with homemade concoctions such as pineapple-weed and mint kombucha. The restaurant is open on selected dates only, so check the website for details.

Ambitious chef-patron Harriet Mansell previously worked with Mark Hix, interned at Noma in Denmark and competed on *Great British Menu*. She also runs sister venue Lilac, just across town, which specialises in small plates and natural wines. It shares the same values (quality, seasonality, locality and sustainability) as the original venue and is a gorgeous spot for an aperitif or to linger over shared plates and good conversation.

Trencherman's tip

Fancy incorporating more wild food into your home cooking? The Robin Wylde team also host foraging walks.

Chef Harriet Mansell | **Tasting menu from** £85 | **Seats** 18

robinwylde.com | 63a Silver Street, Lyme Regis, Dorset, DT7 3HR | 07308 079427

67 Three Horseshoes Pub & Kitchen

Asian-inspired seafood thrills

This 300-year-old thatched pub, in the village of Burton Bradstock on Dorset's Jurassic Coast, exudes charm and won Best Newcomer at the Trencherman's Awards 2022 for its refreshingly unpretentious environment.

Husband-and-wife team Jaap and Hannah Schep met while working for the Marriott group and now delight diners with their own offering. A good proportion of the menu majors on local fish, with Dutch-born chef Jaap especially fond of Pan-Asian flavour profiles: Indonesian seafood curry and tiger-prawn pad thai sit comfortably alongside more British-leaning pub dishes like the seafood ploughman's.

Not to be overlooked is the exciting list of bar snacks which, in quantity, could kick plans for a starter, main and pud into touch. Who wouldn't enjoy working their way through small plates of Dutch bitterballen (beef croquettes), Poole Bay oysters, and tempura pork fillet bao bun with peanut and cucumber salad and fiery sriracha mayo?

The list of by-the-bottle wines has recently doubled while the number available by the glass has also increased, and includes many English sparkling wines and intriguing international drops.

Trencherman's tip

The refurbished garden offers an à la carte menu with full table service, so alfresco diners can receive the same relaxing experience and excellent food as those indoors.

Chef Jaap Schep | **3-course dinner from** £32 | **Seats** 65

threehorseshoesburtonbradstock.co.uk | Mill Street, Burton Bradstock, Dorset, DT6 4QZ | 01308 897259

68 The Seaside Boarding House

Jurassic Coast treasure

Sitting on cliffs overlooking Dorset's sweeping Chesil Beach and Lyme Bay, The Seaside Boarding House is a true treasure on the Jurassic Coast.

Inspired by classic British Edwardian hotels and the Cape Cod paintings of Edward Hopper, this antidote to city life was the brainchild of the creators of London's internationally renowned Groucho Club and exudes the quality you'd expect from such provenance.

It's evidenced no more so than in the restaurant. Whether you're visiting for a simple breakfast, long lunch, intimate dinner for two, or six-course banquet with all the bells and whistles, the menus celebrate modern British cuisine while championing seasonal produce from Dorset's farms, smallholdings and fishing boats. It doesn't

get much more local than Portland crab, paired here with green gazpacho soup and walnut oil.

When the sun's shining, the restaurant's large patio doors are flung open, although on balmy days you might prefer a seat on the terrace overlooking Chesil Beach. It's a popular spot for a signature cocktail, glass of fizz or nightcap under the stars.

Extend your visit with a stay in one of the smart sea-view rooms. Art lovers will be in seventh heaven amid nautical paintings and a collection of Peter Blake prints on loan from a London gallery.

Trencherman's tip

Don't miss cocktail hour – between 5pm and 6pm every day – when selected cocktails and Prosecco are just £5.

Chef Seldon Curry | **3-course dinner from** £60 | **Seats** 60 | **Bedrooms** 9 | **Room rate from** £245

theseasideboardinghouse.com | Cliff Road, Burton Bradstock, Dorset, DT6 4RB | 01308 897205

69 The Club House

Coastal cool at West Bexington

Dining at this Chesil Beach restaurant elicits that 'struck gold' feeling thanks to its unique setting, smart cooking and innovative drinks list.

Set in a 1930s Olympic-pool clubhouse that retains many of its original features, the interiors are best described as mid-century modern meets New England nautical. It's a fitting backdrop for head chef William Hickton's fish-focused menus.

Net-fresh seafood from local fishermen along with produce from nearby farms (including handpicked veggies from the restaurant's own kitchen garden) form the basis of the two-AA-rosette dishes.

Compilations showcasing the uber-local ingredients include West Bay lobster bon bon, Tamarisk Farm crab salad and cod with foraged sea beets.

To elevate the experience further, sommelier Fefe Kovacs is on hand to provide impeccable wine pairings. The Club House is also renowned for its top-tier cocktails so don't leave without sampling a West Bexington Breeze: a luscious blend of Doorly's white rum, Tosolini Limoncello, St-Germain Elderflower Liqueur, lemon juice and rosemary.

The creative concoctions are best sipped on the heated outdoor deck, with its panoramic views of the Jurassic Coast and occasional live jazz sessions in summer.

Trencherman's tip

Visit on a Sunday to devour a two-course roast for a very competitive £20.

Chef William Hickton | **3-course dinner from** £35 | **Seats** 65 | **EV charging**

theclubhousewestbexington.co.uk | 1 Beach Road, West Bexington, Dorset, DT2 9DG | 01308 898302

Best Front of House Team

Crab House Cafe

'Trencherman's puts the South West on a pedestal'

Nigel Bloxham, owner

Left to right: Darren Roberts and Nigel Bloxham of Crab House Cafe
with Penny Coventry of Churchill China (event partner)

70 Crab House Cafe

Sustainable seafood by the shore

Overlooking Dorset's famed Chesil Beach, Crab House Cafe is a rustic and laid-back setting where visitors can feast on seafood plucked from the ocean mere metres away.

Sustainability is paramount at the cafe and owner Nigel Bloxham (who previously supplied fish to Keith Floyd) works closely with local fishermen to source seafood from the surrounding waters, which is usually served the day it's caught. Skate wing, sea bass, lemon sole, gurnard, john dory and plaice are just a glimpse of what's to be discovered on the day's specials board.

The cafe's eponymous crustacean is best enjoyed à deux. Whole Portland brown crab is served simply with dressed salad and mayo, leaving the delicate meat to do all the talking. Arguably the star of the show here, however, are the oysters. Grown at the cafe's own oyster farm just a short paddle from the restaurant, the prized bivalves are fresh, plump and ready to be slurped au naturel.

With so many briny delights on offer there's a good chance you may feel a tad overwhelmed by the menu. Fear not: the stellar staff (and winners of Best Front of House Team at the Trencherman's Awards 2023) will steer you in the right direction.

Trencherman's tip

Pair your seafood with Dorset's Bride Valley Chardonnay. It makes a marvellous match for almost everything on the menu.

Chef George Brace | **3-course dinner from** £34 | **Seats** 43

crabhousecafe.co.uk | Ferryman's Way, Portland Road, Wyke Regis, Dorset, DT4 9YU | 01305 788867

71 The Acorn Inn

Literary-inspired dining

Mentioned in *Tess of the d'Urbervilles* and located in the birthplace of its author Thomas Hardy, The Acorn offers everything you'd expect from a history-steeped English coaching inn. Exposed ceiling beams, oak-panelled walls and roaring log fires all allude to its 16th-century origins, but it's the award-winning restaurant that attracts a contemporary clientele.

Chef Ana Martins compiles menus that capitalise on Dorset's finest seasonal produce while staying refreshingly unpretentious. Local favourites include braised Jurassic Coast pork belly with creamy potatoes, chantenay carrots, spinach and scrumpy jus, and line-caught cod fillet with a crab bisque, savoy cabbage and bacon.

Attempt to save a little room as The Acorn is renowned for its salivation-inducing puddings. Pair the apricot mousse, shortbread crumble and white chocolate compilation with a dessert wine or liqueur from the extensive drinks list.

Trencherman's tip

Those chasing the full coaching inn experience can book a bed for the night in one of ten tastefully decorated guestrooms. Or, if you're simply passing through for the day, grab a bench in the sun-dappled beer garden and tuck into a ploughman's lunch or fish and chips with a pint of local ale or a refreshing gin and tonic.

Chef Ana Martins | **3-course dinner from** £40 | **Seats** 40 | **Bedrooms** 10 | **Room rate from** £140
acorn-inn.co.uk | 28 Fore Street, Evershot, Dorset, DT2 0JW | 01935 83228

72 The Oyster & Fish House

Fish feasting with beautiful bay views

All of the catch on the menus at Mark Hix's Lyme Regis restaurant is caught off the South West coast – often from Lyme Bay itself – so there's a lovely synergy to tucking into the spoils of the sea while gazing at the coast through floor-to-ceiling windows.

The Dorset seafood guru serves pared-back dishes that put beautifully fresh local fish front and centre. Supporting the Lyme Bay Fisheries and Conservation Reserve is one of Mark's top priorities, so guests can expect to find bycatch on the daily line-up.

Seafood is matched with carefully chosen seasonal ingredients sourced from local producers. Dishes like shellfish soup with rouille and croutons, baked Lyme Bay scallops with herb crust, and grilled catch of the day with sea vegetables showcase quality produce minus any pomp or pretension.

The drinks list provides a tour of the region's distillers, craft brewers and vineyards, with headliners Castlewood Vineyard and Bride Valley leading a cast that includes local craft beer brewers Gilt & Flint and Dorset's Black Cow Pure Milk Vodka. Seasonal cocktails also showcase local spirits – try Ven Steadian for a taste of small-batch Black Ven Rum (crafted in Lyme Regis) with Angostura bitters and orange peel.

Trencherman's tip

Check out the regular guest chef events featuring other South West chefs of note. Or, for a more intimate dining experience, book a seat at one of Mark's regular Kitchen Table lunches and dinners which take place in his Charmouth home.

Chef Mark Hix | **3-course dinner from** £30 | **Seats** 40

theoysterandfishhouse.co.uk | Cobb Road, Lyme Regis, Dorset, DT7 3JP | 01297 446910

73 Tom's Lyme Regis

Briny delights by the sea

Coastal resorts don't come much prettier than Lyme Regis with its picturesque promenade overlooking the historic Cobb. Tom's Lyme Regis has a covetable spot just a stone's throw from the water, meaning the boat-to-plate journey of its sought-after seafood is mere yards.

Lyme Bay scallops, prawns and crab jostle for pole position in a seafood-laden menu that also often features rock oysters and Dorset Blue lobster. Not sure which to go for? Tom's Fish Board for two features the lot, served alongside creamy saffron aioli, hunks of freshly baked bread and triple-cooked chips.

When the weather plays ball, sit on the oceanfront terrace with a glass of fizz from nearby Castlewood Vineyard and enjoy a light bite from the new lunchtime favourites menu. Lyme Bay crab sandwiches and

devilled mackerel served with Isle of Wight tomatoes are perpetual crowd-pleasers.

There are options to satisfy meat eaters and vegetarians here too, but really it's the seafood that's the draw, with a line-up that changes daily to reflect the day's catch. Indeed, it's not unusual for Tom to take delivery of a freshly caught haul in the afternoon, which is then hastily added to that evening's menu.

Trencherman's tip

Leave room for pudding. Tom's chocolate mousse is the stuff of local legend.

Chef Tom Robinson | **3-course dinner from** £37 | **Seats** 28

tomslymeregis.com | Marine Parade, Lyme Regis, Dorset, DT7 3JQ | 01297 816018

74 WestBeach

Alfresco seafood suppers

Dorset staycationers and locals strolling Bournemouth's picturesque promenade are instinctively lured into family-owned WestBeach restaurant.

Sunshine spills on the epicureans who dine on fruits de mer sharing platters and sip refreshing cocktails on the smart deck overlooking golden sands and clean waves.

While the alfresco eating is a major draw, inside offers an equal feast for the senses. If you don't score a table by the window, avert your gaze from the sea to the team of innovative chefs crafting flavourful creations in the design-led open kitchen.

Fresh fish and seafood are the star attractions, and the catch from local waters around Bournemouth and Poole forms the bedrock of the enticing menu.

Choose from crowd-pleasers such as plump mussels bathed in white wine, garlic, cream and shallots, oven-roasted catch of the day swathed in lemon and thyme, or lobster brushed with chilli and lime butter. And, of course, there's no shame in embracing the classic British fave of golden beer-battered fish and chips with mushy peas and tartare sauce.

An exciting wine list, with bottles sourced from all over the world, makes it easy to pair your pick of the menu with a perfect match.

Trencherman's tip

Planning a sunrise sea swim? There's no better place than WestBeach to refuel afterwards with its next-level views and brekkie. The crab benedict is an excellent choice, as is a Smoky Mary breakfast cocktail.

Chef Andras Veres | **3-course dinner from** £50 | **Seats** 100

west-beach.co.uk | Pier Approach, Bournemouth, Dorset, BH2 5AA | 01202 587785

75 Captain's Club Hotel & Spa

Stylish riverside retreat

In a town best known for its historic castle and quaint cottages, the Captain's Club's floor-to-ceiling windows and contemporary furnishings create a refreshingly modern vibe.

At its restaurant, chef Mo Sabbir excels in modern British dishes executed with precision. Pan-seared chicken breast stuffed with wild sorrel and truffle mousse served with herb-crushed potatoes and sautéed spinach, or rack of lamb with hasselback potatoes and minted pea puree are as agreeable to the eye as they are to the palate.

The hotel has everything needed for a relaxing weekend break. Indulge in treatments and pampering at the spa or pootle along the river to the coast for an invigorating dose of sea air. Then, ease into the evening with cocktails in the lounge followed by dinner at the Club Restaurant.

In summer, reserve a spot on the sun-strewn terrace to relish a sparkling afternoon tea or consume ocean-fresh shellfish — such as Poole Bay oysters — with a glass of crisp Champagne.

Trencherman's tip

Oenophiles will enjoy the carefully selected drops from sommelier Corey Evans' enticing new wine list.

Chef Mohammed Sabbir | **3-course dinner from** £35 | **Seats** 120
Bedrooms 29 | **Room rate from** £280 | **EV charging**

captainsclubhotel.com | Wick Ferry, Christchurch, Dorset, BH23 1HU | 01202 475111

Somerset, Bristol & Bath

Restaurants listed in the guide correspond to the numbers plotted on the map.

All locations are approximate

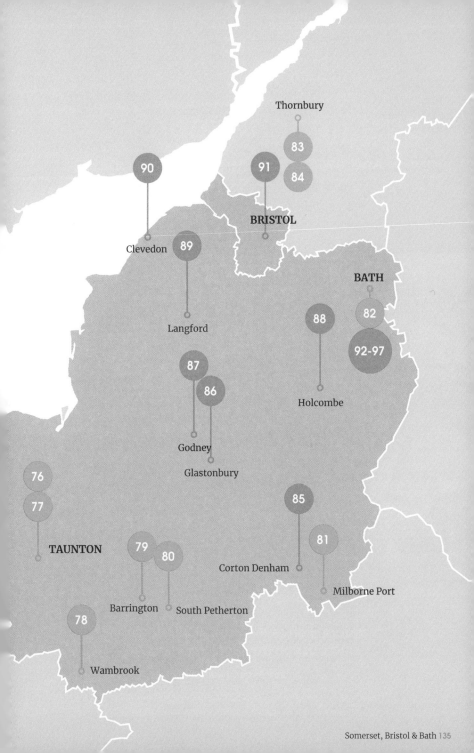

Thornbury

83

91 84

BRISTOL

90

Clevedon

89

BATH

Langford

82

88 92-97

87

86 Holcombe

Godney

Glastonbury

76

85

77 81

TAUNTON

79

80 Corton Denham

Milborne Port

Barrington South Petherton

78

Wambrook

Best Trencherman's Chef

Andrew Swann, The Castle at Taunton

'It's recognition of the hard work, dedication
and passion my team and I put in'

Andrew Swann, head chef

Left to right: Andrew Swann of The Castle at Taunton, Mark Hix (host)
and Jon Harris of Hallgarten & Novum Wines (award sponsor)

76 The Castle at Taunton

Stylish dining in the heart of town

Perennially popular, this wisteria-covered hotel in the heart of Taunton is renowned for its timeless elegance and award-winning culinary flair.

The Castle has seen a number of talented chefs pass through its kitchen, and now head chef Andrew Swann oversees its buzzing restaurants and private dining rooms.

The main restaurant, Brazz, is open for brunch and lunch, but really comes to life during dinner service when low-level lighting and leather banquette seating create an intimate atmosphere. Quality South West ingredients form the backbone of the menu, and guests can expect to find the likes of Brixham crab and prawn roulade, pickled mouli, lobster and dill sauce, and Quantock lamb rump and crispy belly with salsa verde, creamed potatoes and purple sprouting.

The past year has seen the refurbishment and launch of The Drawing Room, a relaxed lounge area where hotel guests and visitors can book in for afternoon tea or a light lunch, or enjoy an evening cocktail. Formal restaurant Castle Bow has reverted to a private dining space, hosting weddings and celebrations in glamorous art deco surroundings.

Trencherman's tip

Head to Brazz for Twilight Hour (between 11pm and midnight) on Fridays and Saturdays to enjoy two-for-one cocktails and house spirits.

Chef Andrew Swann | **3-course dinner from** £35 | **Seats** 70
Bedrooms 44 | **Room rate from** £120 | **EV charging**
the-castle-hotel.com | Castle Green, Taunton, Somerset, TA1 1NF | 01823 272671

77 Augustus

Smart courtyard bistro

This glass-fronted bistro is hidden within an intimate courtyard away from the hubbub of Taunton's town centre, so could easily be missed were it not for its stellar reputation.

Augustus enjoys a loyal following of customers who frequent it for its high-calibre cooking in unpretentious surroundings. It's even been described by *Observer* critic Jay Rayner as '*a classy bistro that will look after you and make the world feel just that little bit better*'.

For over a decade, owners Richard Guest and Cedric Chirossel have proved that the hallmarks of a consistently good restaurant are first-rate front-of-house service and quality ingredients.

Richard's cooking style leans towards classic French cuisine while also celebrating seasonal British produce. Popular dishes include Devon smoked eel and scrambled egg with curried oil and smoked herring caviar; homemade rabbit faggots with summer greens, gratin potato and onion gravy; and slow-roasted duck with pommes anna, beetroots, carrots and courgettes.

Richard and Cedric are dedicated supporters of independent local businesses so most of the ingredients are sourced nearby, with fresh fruit and veg from greengrocer Granny Smiths and Pitney Farm, salads from Capland Acre, Brixham-caught fish from Phil Bowditch and meat from Riverside Butchers.

Chef Richard Guest | **3-course dinner from** £35 | **Seats** 40

augustustaunton.co.uk | 3 The Courtyard, St James Street, Taunton, Somerset, TA1 1JR | 01823 324354

78 The Cotley Inn

Beautiful food in an AONB

An evening on The Cotley Inn's south-facing terrace provides a banquet for the senses: bees buzz around lavender, delicious smells emanate from flavourful dishes and a visual feast is provided by the lush fields in which much of the food was grown and reared.

The Grade II-listed country inn sits in the heart of the Cotley Estate in the Blackdown Hills and has been exquisitely updated in contemporary farmhouse style by owners Maddie Beaumont and Ben Porter.

Being part of an estate gives head chef Dan Brown access to an abundance of ultra-fresh produce such as Ruby Red beef, rare-breed pork and chicken, and veg from the kitchen garden. His nose-to-tail cooking style aligns with Maddie and Ben's sustainability principles, so there are often home-smoked meats and less conventional cuts to try.

Dan began his career with *MasterChef* winner Mat Follas at The Wild Garlic in Dorset. At The Cotley he crafts modern interpretations of pub classics for a pleasingly pared-back menu, which includes dishes such as Wambrook lamb rump with pea and mint puree, salt and pepper Jersey Royals, and sesame-dressed broccoli with wild garlic and lemongrass.

Four country-chic bedrooms make this a delicious location for a stopover. Book in to explore the wine list and wake up to the mooing of the cows in the field next door.

Trencherman's tip

Visit for alfresco dining in summer, when sourdough pizzas and small plates packed with locally sourced fare are served from a tin hut in the sunny garden.

Chefs Dan Brown and Danny Baker | **3-course dinner from** £38 | **Seats** 60
Bedrooms 4 | **Room rate from** £135

cotleyinnwambrook.co.uk | Wambrook, Chard, Somerset, TA20 3EN | 01460 62348

79 The Barrington Boar

Refined comfort food

When Alasdair Clifford returned to his home county of Somerset in 2018, he brought with him a host of skills honed in top restaurants such as Chez Bruce in London. They've been put to good use in the friendly environment of this contemporary country pub, which he runs in partnership with his wife Victoria Collins.

On taking over the Boar, the duo refreshed the pub's interior and menu to create a stylish setting in which to serve *'refined comfort food'* – a modest description for something that's nudged its way into the Estrella Damm Top 100 Gastropubs.

These gratifying dishes offer a taste of the local terroir – an example being charcoal-grilled fillet of 40-day aged Devon Red Ruby beef from Meadow Lea Farm (near South Petherton) served with hand-cut chips, smoked ox cheek and mushroom croquette, black garlic and parsley salad.

As well as working closely with local farmers, foragers and cheesemongers, the couple also collaborate with regional breweries and host an ever-evolving collection of ales, ciders and spirits.

Exciting times are afoot this year with the acquisition of a large site next door. Subject to planning, the couple intend to build a bakery, further accommodation and a market garden (including native Somerset fruit trees) to supply the kitchen.

Trencherman's tip

Match your meal with a bottle of Smith & Evans sparkling wine, made just a few miles away.

Chef Alasdair Clifford | **3-course dinner from** £36.55 | **Seats** 45
Bedrooms 4 | **Room rate from** £113

thebarringtonboar.co.uk | Main Street, Barrington, Ilminster, Somerset, TA19 0JB | 01460 259281

80 Holm

South London meets rural Somerset

Over the past few years, an influx of London chefs and restaurateurs have made their way west, swapping the city's bright lights for the South West's big skies, coastlines and greenery.

Nicholas Balfe – part of the trio who established esteemed London restaurants Salon, Levan and Larry's – joined the exodus at the end of 2021 to launch Holm in his home county of Somerset.

Connecting to the land and local people is the driving force behind this contemporary restaurant, which is housed within a former bank in South Petherton. The fields surrounding the small town supply many of the ingredients that contribute to the ever-evolving menus. Nicholas is careful to partner with farmers, growers, butchers, gamekeepers and fishermen who share his respect for and love of quality ingredients.

The open-plan dining room is accented with mid-century modern furniture and interesting artwork, providing a casual setting for the team's slick food. The focus of each dish is very much on the beauty of the ingredients, which shine in dishes like Cornish pollack with peas and cider butter, and ham-hock croquette with little gem lettuce.

A select and sensibly priced wine list showcases low-intervention, biodynamic and organic wines from small-scale producers – best enjoyed on the outdoor terrace.

Trencherman's tip

Seven boutique bedrooms are due to be completed this year, transforming this Somerset find into a rural dine-and-stay destination.

Chef Nicholas Balfe | **3-course dinner from** £30 | **Seats** 30 inside, 30 outside
holmsomerset.co.uk | 28 St James Street, South Petherton, Somerset, TA13 5BW | 01460 712470

81 The Clockspire Restaurant and Bar

Great food in grand surroundings

A visit to The Clockspire is like stepping into a bygone era, thanks to its 19th-century school building setting of vaulted oak-beamed ceilings, polished stone floors and candelabras hanging from the rafters.

In the kitchen, head chef Luke Sutton (who started his career at Michelin-starred L'Ortolan in Berkshire) creates elegant modern British dishes that befit this opulent setting.

Smoked chicken thigh with sweetcorn, girolles and leek oil, and beef tartare with wild garlic and pickled shallots, are a snapshot of the starters on offer, while mains are centred around hero ingredients such as Creedy Carver chicken and Cornish bass fillet, often paired with foraged finds from the surrounding countryside.

Special occasion? Gather a group and opt for the tasting menu, aptly named A Taste of the Clockspire, for a memorable evening of exceptional wining and dining.

For those who like to start the evening with an aperitif, there's a sleek marble-topped bar on a mezzanine level over the main restaurant. It's a lush setting for enjoying a pre-dinner glass of Champagne or seasonal cocktail.

Trencherman's tip

On the last Thursday of each month, The Clockspire hosts jazz sessions for those who fancy a side of bebop with dinner.

Chef Luke Sutton | **3-course dinner from** £32 | **Seats** 60

theclockspire.com | Gainsborough, Sherborne, Dorset, DT9 5BA | 01963 251458

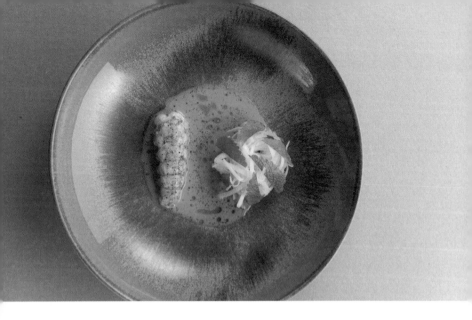

82 The Olive Tree Restaurant

Michelin mastery at Bath's big hitter

This chic restaurant below Bath's boutique Queensberry Hotel needs little introduction, thanks to its impressive accolades (three AA rosettes and a Michelin star for five consecutive years) and inventive menus from Trencherman's Award-winning executive chef Chris Cleghorn.

For the best part of a decade, dedicated gourmets have made the pilgrimage to the Georgian city to delight in course after course of Chris' complex dishes.

Each plate focuses on a core British ingredient, which is complemented by an array of unusual extras. English rhubarb, for example, is paired with a Szechuan meringue, Ivy House sour cream and preserved rose, while Isle of Skye langoustine is coupled with kohlrabi, Tahitian vanilla and

lemon balm. These unexpected fusions of flavour never fail to excite and surprise.

Precede dinner with drinks in the hotel's hip Old Q Bar, which has an inventive cocktail menu inspired by classic tipples from bygone eras. If you love rum, plump for a Hemingway Daiquiri – a refreshing concoction of Devon's Two Drifters white rum, grapefruit, lime and Luxardo Maraschino.

Trencherman's tip

Follow the spectacular dining experience with a comfortable night's slumber by booking a room in one of the hotel's chic guest suites.

Chef Chris Cleghorn | **6-course dinner from** £125 | **Seats** 42 | **Bedrooms** 29 | **Room rate from** £135

olivetreebath.co.uk | 4-7 Russell Street, Bath, BA1 2QF | 01225 447928

83 Ronnie's of Thornbury

Relaxed luxury near Bristol

The discerning diners of Thornbury rejoiced when chef Ron Faulkner opened this refined-yet-rustic dining venture in 2007, as it's the type of exceptional neighbourhood restaurant every foodie dreams of having in their home town.

Ronnie scoured the South West for the perfect spot to establish his first venue which, it transpired, wasn't a buzzy restaurant in one of the big cities but a Grade II-listed former schoolhouse in the market town of Thornbury.

In the 16 years since, Ronnie and team have built a loyal following for their polished, modern British food which showcases local, seasonal ingredients. The evening tasting menu is the restaurant's star attraction and takes diners on a culinary adventure with dishes like line-caught sea bass with

asparagus, samphire, brown shrimp and saffron aioli. There are two-course (£45) and three-course (£55) à la carte options too, but the tasting menu is such good value at £65 that you'd be foolish to pass on the offer.

Wine is another of the chef's great passions, so naturally there's a superb wine list and flight to match the food. Expect to find a healthy selection of English bottles on the line-up (the Woodchester Valley Cuvée is particularly special and produced just 20 miles away), as well as more eclectic finds from lesser-known regions and countries.

Trencherman's tip

Other excuses to visit Ronnie's are the next-level Sunday lunch and the express menu of three informal lunch courses.

Chef Ronnie Faulkner | **3-course dinner from** £55 | **Seats** 36

ronnies-restaurant.co.uk | 11 St Mary Street, Thornbury, Bristol, BS35 2AB | 01454 411137

84 Thornbury Castle

Tudor splendour on the outskirts of Bristol

Dine in historic opulence at this Relais & Châteaux hotel in a castle once owned by King Henry VIII.

Retaining many of its period features, and sympathetically furnished with antiques and fabrics that capture a bygone age, Thornbury Castle will appeal to those who enjoy a sense of occasion and grandiosity with their dining experience. The oak-panelled walls of the 16th-century dining room are lined with gilt-framed paintings of the castle's former patrons, while guestrooms are bedecked with palatial four-poster beds and ornate chandeliers.

Befitting this royal setting, executive chef Carl Cleghorn creates refined dishes fit for a king, maximising the use of locally sourced and castle-grown produce. Whether opting for the à la carte or tasting menu, it's impossible not to be bowled over by the likes of Creedy Carver duck leg and aerated foie gras served with rhubarb, hibiscus and ginger bread, or pan-fried turbot paired with a silky pomme puree, fennel and bouillabaisse sauce.

Elevate the experience further by asking the front-of-house team to help pair the chosen dishes with wine from the extensive list.

Trencherman's tip

Follow afternoon tea in the dining room with a stroll in the castle's beautiful gardens.

Chef Carl Cleghorn | **6-course tasting menu** £110 | **Seats** 50
Bedrooms 26 | **Room rate from** £259 | **EV charging**

thornburycastle.co.uk | Castle Street, Thornbury, Bristol, BS35 1HH | 01454 281182

85 The Queen's Arms

Elevated pub dining

Just about everything on the menu at The Queen's Arms is made from scratch, in-house – from the celery salt sprinkled on the Bloody Marys to the pork scratchings devoured at the bar and the milk buns sandwiching dry-aged beef burgers.

Straddling the Dorset-Somerset border, the pub has a longstanding reputation for its use of homegrown ingredients. Yet when the Mackenzie-Francis family took over in 2021, they worked with head chef Rich Townsend to ramp the homemade ethos up a notch. Now, if something can feasibly be made in The Queen's Arms kitchen, it is – resulting in a charmingly rustic menu of hyper-seasonal dishes.

What Rich and his team can't craft themselves is sourced from quality local producers, including Montgomery Cheddar in North Cadbury and pork from The Story Pig

in Sherborne. Expect to sample elevated pub dishes such as pork collar with grilled runner beans, chorizo and red pepper sauce and crispy pork skin, and salt-baked carrot with crisp kale, chickpea panisse, chermoula and smoked almonds.

Above the pub lie five bedrooms, individually decorated with handpicked antiques and fabrics from the likes of Colefax and Fowler. There's also pooch-friendly accommodation (a two-bedroom cottage and three rooms in The Coach House) for those visiting with a furry friend in tow. Stay the night to explore the many local walkways surrounding the pub, and a drinks list that includes cocktails such as the Somerset Sour (three-year-old cider brandy, Angostura bitters, lemon juice, sugar and egg white).

Chef Rich Townsend | **3-course dinner from** £45 | **Seats** 60
Bedrooms 10 | **Room rate from** £140 | **EV charging**

thequeensarms.com | Corton Denham, Sherborne, Somerset, DT9 4LR | 01963 220317

86 Queen of Cups

Modern Middle Eastern fare in a historic pub setting

A pub in the heart of Glastonbury isn't the first place you'd expect to find some of the best Middle Eastern food in the country, but Queen of Cups is full of surprises.

Leiths graduate Ayesha Kalaji relocated to the Somerset town from London (where she cooked at Bubala, The Good Egg and The Palomar) to establish her own restaurant with friend and business partner Mary-Elizabeth O'Neill.

The duo poured their creative energy into the historic pub on Northload Street, creating a beautiful space to match Ayesha's innovative cooking. Drawing on her Jordanian heritage and French training, she crafts genuinely unique dishes that dazzle with their bold flavours and bright colours. Falafel, for example, is elevated with laverbread (a nod to her North Wales upbringing), sumac, lime, fennel and tahini.

Sourcing seasonally and locally is vital to this (mostly) female kitchen team. All of the meat comes from Stephens Butchers next door and most of the fruit, veg and herbs are sourced from small farms within five miles of the restaurant. As a result, the menu – which is split into nibbles, cold and hot dishes – changes regularly.

An intriguing wine list showcases lesser-known vineyards and local wineries such as Mowbarton Estate and Glastonbury Vineyard.

Trencherman's tip

Over-order on the dips and flatbreads and take leftovers home for later. The team have a stack of biodegradable containers ready and waiting.

Chef Ayesha Kalaji | **3-course dinner from** £36 | **Seats** 45

queenofcups.co.uk | 10–12 Northload Street, Glastonbury, Somerset, BA6 9JJ | 01458 831255

87 The Sheppey Inn

Funky country pub with hidden depths

Farm workers on the Somerset Levels have lubricated their thirsty throats at this Godney pub for centuries, and when Tamsin and Ben Costigan took over The Sheppey in 2020 they were determined to maintain its position at the heart of the community. A renovation with eclectic materials and furnishings, paired with superior food, have seen the duo realise their dream.

The Sheppey is a dark horse. Its exterior gives no hint of the wonders within: part cider house, part boutique hotel. Low-beamed ceilings in the bar contrast with high white walls in the barn. There are cosy booths, regular art exhibitions championing local talent, 1950s retro furniture and guitars waiting to be played. Music matters here – evidenced in the background mix of jazz, funk and blues playing while you dine, and the live bands that grace the stage.

In the kitchen, head chef Tom Ollis whips up modern European food with a Somerset twist. Try local beef with yorkshire pudding and red wine gravy, followed by an ever-evolving line-up of inventive desserts served with a side of homemade ice cream.

Accompanying the food are fine wines, a changing roster of beers and ales (APA Sunshine Reggae from Somerton is a local favourite), and a bar stocked with knock-your-socks-off cask ciders.

Trencherman's tip

A long-decked terrace hanging above the river provides the perfect perch for summer lounging. Look out for voles, kingfishers and even otters amid the idyllic countryside setting.

Chef Tom Ollis | **3-course dinner from** £40 | **Seats** 90 | **Bedrooms** 3 | **Room rate from** £110

thesheppey.co.uk | Lower Godney, Wells, Somerset, BA5 1RZ | 01458 831594

88 The Holcombe

Eco-savvy dining in Somerset

The Holcombe is a labour of love for owners Alan and Caroline Lucas, whose kitchen garden inspires the imaginative menus they craft for one of the most environmentally conscious restaurants in the country.

The 17th-century inn is surrounded by two acres of land that is the source of fruit, veg, herbs and flowers for The Holcombe's uber-seasonal menus. What can't be cultivated on-site is sourced from local producers.

Sustainability-wise, Alan and Caroline set themselves a high bar. All food waste is composted and used cooking oil becomes biodiesel. There are also wildlife-friendly plots among the raised beds, while 40,000 bees are kept to produce honey.

In the kitchen, Alan is a one-man prepping, pickling and preserving machine, and relishes finding creative new ways to use the produce from his plots and polytunnel. It's

his passion to ensure everything – from the sourdough bagels at breakfast to the ricotta-style cheese at dinner and the ice cream served with pudding – is made in-house.

Flavour-packed dishes include the likes of tandoor-roasted cauliflower with white onion puree, spiced lentils and toasted almonds, and Creedy Carver duck breast with red cabbage and quince puree.

After dinner, sit in the covered Mediterranean-style garden to relish views over Downside Abbey with a house-infused gin (the elderflower is a must-try).

Trencherman's tip

Book one of the gorgeous rural-luxe guestrooms or dog-friendly lodges to extend your visit.

Chef Alan Lucas | **3-course dinner from** £45 | **Seats** 45 | **Bedrooms** 11 | **Room rate from** £170

theholcombe.com | Stratton Road, Holcombe, Somerset, BA3 5EB | 01761 232478

89 The Langford Inn

Dog-friendly coaching inn

This characterful 17th-century coaching inn on the outskirts of Bristol is popular with locals and attracts a steady stream of travellers looking for sustenance en route to Bristol Airport, just five miles away.

The pub is owned by Butcombe Brewery, based in the neighbouring village of Wrington, so there's a cracking range of cask ales and beers on tap. This weaves its way into the daily menus too, such as in the Butcombe Gold beer-battered fish and chips.

Having recently secured two AA rosettes, chef Ryan Granaski is adept at creating dishes that showcase locally sourced produce. Plates such as salt-baked beetroot with sprouting broccoli tempura, lentil dal, smoked tomato jam and a cumin and coconut yogurt, and kimchi and wild rice fritters with black sesame hummus, rose harissa carrots and cashew dukkah give an indication of a chef unafraid of transcending traditional pub staples.

The inn was recently refurbished and has seven boutique bedrooms decorated in a contemporary country-chic style. With the rolling Mendip Hills on its doorstep and dogs welcome overnight too, it's a perfect spot for a gourmet weekend away.

Trencherman's tip

The Langford is a true community hub so keep an eye on socials for upcoming events such as its monthly supper clubs.

Chef Ryan Granaski | **3-course dinner from** £30 | **Seats** 76 | **Bedrooms** 7 | **Room rate from** £94

butcombe.com/the-langford-inn-somerset | Langford Road, Langford, Somerset, BS40 5BL | 01934 446059

90 Murrays of Clevedon

Authentic taste of Italy

Whet the appetite for Italian-inspired dining by starting your visit to Murrays with a perusal of its shelves laden with lemons from Amalfi, prosciutto from Emilia-Romagna, and extra virgin olive oil from Sicily.

Fine artisanal produce is the beating heart of this family-run restaurant, deli and wine shop. Run by Reuben Murray (youngest son of founders Gail and John), the business has served locals and visitors to the Victorian seaside town of Clevedon for almost 40 years.

It's not just deli customers who get to delight in the quality ingredients; diners at the restaurant are also lucky beneficiaries. Imported foods are paired with seasonal South West produce, including fresh Cornish fish, to create Italian-style dishes with contemporary flair.

Plump for a selection of cicchetti to start – highlights include the beef bresaola with crispy roasted roman artichokes, Amalfi lemon mayo and capers, and charred long-stem broccoli with cumin, chilli, buffalo mozzarella and toasted almonds.

The line-up of mains includes the likes of handmade pasta, chicken milanese with potato rosti and spiced Sicilian tomato polpa, and aubergine parmigiano. Or keep it casual with authentic Italian pizza made with San Marzano tomatoes and fior di latte.

Trencherman's tip

Hosting a private event? Book Enoteca at Murrays, a space inspired by Gail's Italian courtyard and her love of good food and Italian sunshine.

Chefs Chris Sheppard and Reuben Murray | **3-course dinner from** £25 | **Seats** 40

murraysofclevedon.co.uk | 91 Hill Road, Clevedon, Somerset, BS21 7PN | 01275 341222

91 Harbour House

Rustic riverside dining

On balmy summer evenings in Bristol, few restaurants can compete with Harbour House's waterside location for post-work drinks against a backdrop of paddleboarders and kayakers.

The building that Harbour House calls home (and which was formerly Severnshed) is said to have been designed by Isambard Kingdom Brunel and used as his private boathouse.

In its latest incarnation, it's a pleasingly rustic restaurant with vaulted ceilings and verdant tropical plants which create a relaxed and airy vibe. This informality extends to the food offering, which majors on all-day dining.

Freshly caught seafood is the star of chef Altin Ndoja's line-up, executed simply but exquisitely in dishes like seafood linguine, fish cakes, smoked mackerel salad, and fish and chips.

Meat eaters needn't feel left out, however, as there's also a stellar selection of piscine-free options including grilled Gloucestershire lamb cutlets with apricot harissa couscous, baba ganoush and gremolata. Vegetarians are catered for with the likes of orzo accompanied by roasted onion puree, charred courgette, and king oyster and porcini mushrooms.

Trencherman's tip

Pair your meal with a glass of something bubbly from the Britz list, Harbour House's curation of sparkling wines from British vineyards.

Chef Altin Ndoja | **3-course dinner from** £30 | **Seats** 100

hhbristol.com | The Grove, Bristol, BS1 4RB | 01179 251212

92 The Circus Restaurant

European chic in Bath city centre

Situated between the Bath landmarks of The Circus and The Royal Crescent, in a golden-stone Georgian townhouse, The Circus Restaurant exudes the city's historic splendour – minus the pomp and pretension.

The family-run establishment specialises in modern European cooking and seasonally changing menus, accompanied by Old World wines. It's a year-round hit with locals and has a bustling atmosphere, particularly in the summer months when guests can dine alfresco at the smattering of on-street tables.

Light summer starters – such as Iford Manor cured ham with burrata, nectarine and heritage tomato salad, and Brixham sea bass cured with mango and lime gin – prime the palate for a curated selection of French-inspired mains punctuated by hero ingredients from the South West.

French-trimmed guinea fowl supreme is served with goat's cheese arancini, courgette ribbons and roasted peach, while herb-crusted pork tenderloin is paired with buckwheat, braised ham hock, peas and broad beans.

The sweet-toothed will relish zingy desserts such as the lemon and elderflower posset with lemon curd, crushed Ricciarelli biscuits and lemon verbena.

Trencherman's tip

Book in for a lazy lunch to enjoy the extremely good value set menu over a bottle of England's only home-produced Crémant from Bride Valley in Dorset.

Chef Tom Smith | **3-course dinner from** £37 | **Seats** 60

thecircusrestaurant.co.uk | 34 Brock Street, Bath, BA1 2LN | 01225 466020

93 The Beckford Bottle Shop

Bistro chic in Bath

Established in 2015, The Beckford Bottle Shop is a firm fixture on Bath's culinary circuit. Initially the delicious secret of locals and savvy visitors, its cover was well and truly blown when *Observer* critic Jay Rayner gave it a glowing review in 2022 – the same year it picked up Best Restaurant at the Food Reader Awards.

Like all Beckford Group venues, this bijou bistro and wine merchant makes a point of doing simple things well. Head chef James Harris spends his weekends foraging for the freshest produce, from which he crafts ingredient-led small plates with a focus on flavour over frills. Think Bath chaps with Bramley apple, cured ChalkStream trout with fennel and wild garlic flowers, and epic charcuterie boards, accompanied by a wine from the superb collection in the adjoining bottle shop.

From impromptu lunches to milestone celebrations, any occasion is amplified at this effortlessly cool setting which features tin-clad ceilings and Chesterfield sofas.

Winter dinners are best devoured in the basement dining room with its low lighting, dark wood and original features. In summer, guests can graze on local artisan cheeses, charcuterie and wines by the glass under the alfresco awning.

Trencherman's tip

Stroll down the road to check out new sister venue Beckford Canteen, which opened in a former Georgian greenhouse in January 2023. Dine at the window countertop for the ultimate people-watching perch.

Chef James Harris | **3-course dinner from** £25 | **Seats** 60

beckfordbottleshop.com | 5-8 Saville Row, Bath, BA1 2QP | 01225 809302

94 Robun

Creative Japanese cooking

This smart restaurant in the heart of Bath offers a refreshing alternative to the city's many brasseries and brunch spots. Crafting a modern take on Japanese yakiniku (the art of grilling meat, seafood and vegetables over a traditional robata charcoal fire), Robun has made a name for itself as one of the region's most exciting dining spots.

New head chef Kasae Fraser worked in restaurants around the world, including Michelin-starred Operakällaren in Stockholm, before taking up the role at Robun in 2023.

Cult Japanese classics like sushi and tempura feature on his menus, but it's the more creative dishes (think wagyu beef tataki with yuzu ponzu dressing, and black cod with den miso marinade) that excite the ambitious chef.

Make an evening reservation to get stuck into his à la carte menu of small plates, signature ensembles and robata dishes, or take a lunchtime trip to work your way through a bento box of delicious bites – meat, veg and seafood varieties are available.

Whenever you visit, it's worth taking public transport in order to make the most of the unique drinks menu. The cocktail list is extremely good and features intriguing concoctions, including the Doki Doki of pisco, strawberry syrup, elderflower cordial, Yuzushu, cold brew jasmine tea and egg white.

Trencherman's tip

The sake menu is one of the most extensive in the South West and includes fine examples of rice wine, from the fresh and fruity to the unfiltered and rice-centric.

Chef Kasae Fraser | **3-course dinner from** £29 | **Seats** 76

robun.co.uk | 4 Princes Buildings, George Street, Bath, BA1 2ED | 01225 614424

95 Corkage

Convivial dining in the heart of Bath

Corkage embodies the rustic charm of a continental neighbourhood bistro, exuding a cosy intimacy where you're on first-name terms with the team and can ask questions without inhibition.

Originally a pop-up venture conceived by pals Richard Knighting and Marty Grant, it's now one of Bath's most coveted and award-winning dining destinations. The premise is simple: a rotation of seasonal plates paired with a handpicked curation of wines, available by the glass or bottle. If you're bowled over by a particular drop, you can pick up a bottle to take home.

When the pair opened Corkage, they aimed to create a place of conviviality and conversation. Sharing is actively encouraged, so don't be shy about ordering multiple plates from the creative line-up. Conveniently split into veggie, fish and meat dishes, the ever-evolving menu features the likes of salmon kilawin with crème fraîche, orange and radish, and charred tenderstem with yuzu dressing, cashew milk and brined grapes.

While the food is of an exceedingly high calibre (Richard has been a chef for over 20 years, having trained in Marco Pierre White and Jean-Georges Vongerichten kitchens in London), it's taken to another level with the addition of Richard and Marty's other love: wine. The duo's oenophilia and instinct for pairing is exceptional, so take the opportunity to sample something new.

Trencherman's tip

Visit on a Friday to enjoy a set lunch with a glass of house wine at £20 for two courses or £25 for three – best eaten alfresco in the expansive heated courtyard, where verdant foliage instantly transports guests to sunnier climes.

Chefs Richard Knighting and Vincent Gatay | **3-course dinner from** £35 | **Seats** 55

corkagebath.com | 5 Chapel Row, Bath, BA1 1HN | 01225 423417

Chez Dominique

Parisian charm overlooking the River Avon

This family-owned restaurant has established itself as a firm favourite in well-heeled Bath. It occupies a prime spot close to Pulteney Bridge, one of the most photographed examples of Georgian architecture in the city, and has a private dining room overlooking the weir.

Husband-and-wife owners Chris Tabbitt and Sarah Olivier opened the doors in 2016, and named it after their first child, Dominic. Today, it radiates French bistro charm, reflecting Chris' training in classic French and British cuisines at quality establishments including Bibendum in London's Michelin House.

Chez Dominique head chef Sam Lewis uses the freshest South West ingredients to create a seasonal menu bursting with classic flavours and techniques. His contemporary European cooking is matched by the modern decor.

It doesn't get much more continental than onglet steak, a cut beloved by French chefs but largely overlooked this side of La Manche. At Chez Dominique it's served with mustard and tarragon butter and pommes frites. Keep it français for dessert with a crémeux au chocolat with hazelnut, dulce de leche and a lemon and ginger tuille.

The wine list features robust French classics alongside stunning New World varieties. Add warm, friendly and attentive service and you'll be so relaxed that you'll leave expecting to step into gay Paris rather than Jane Austen's Bath.

Trencherman's tip

Book a table at lunchtime to take advantage of the set-price menu. Four-legged friends are welcome too.

Chef Sam Lewis | **3-course dinner from** £34 | **Seats** 40

chezdominique.co.uk | 15 Argyle Street, Bath, BA2 4BQ | 01225 463482

97 Yak Yeti Yak

Home-style Nepalese cuisine

When Sarah and Sera Gurung decided to settle in the UK in 2004, they followed their instincts and opened the UK's first purely Nepalese restaurant in the basement of one of Bath's grand Georgian townhouses.

Inspired by the couple's travels and evenings spent in small Himalayan tea shops enjoying meals cooked by some of the world's lesser-known culinary heroes, Yak Yeti Yak was a place for them to share the food they loved. The unique offering was a hit with the locals, so much so that within a couple of years they moved the restaurant to a roomier basement on Pierrepont Street.

'Our food is a mixture of typical Nepalese home-style cooking and off-the-beaten-track tea shop meals,' says Sarah. *'The simplicity of everyday Nepalese food is something we think should be celebrated.'*

Everything is cooked by Sarah and Sera in the Yak Yeti Yak kitchen – from the handmade pork momos to the chutneys and marinades. The main menu remains consistent throughout the year, but seasonal specials are chalked up on the board for returning diners who want to mix things up. Staying true to Nepalese cuisine, around half of the dishes are vegetarian or vegan.

Trencherman's tip

Choose between conventional tables and chairs, floor-level tables with cushions, or alfresco dining in the courtyard.

Chefs Sarah and Sera Gurung | **3-course dinner from** £26 | **Seats** 60

yakyetiyak.co.uk | 12 Pierrepont Street, Bath, BA1 1LA | 01225 442299

Wiltshire

Restaurants listed in the guide correspond to the numbers plotted on the map.

All locations are approximate

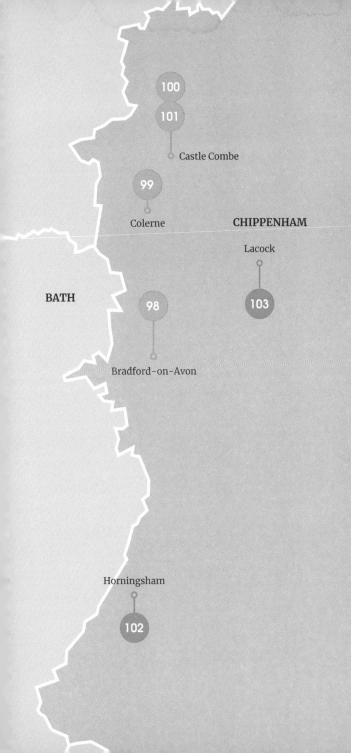

100
101
Castle Combe

99
Colerne

CHIPPENHAM

Lacock

103

BATH

98
Bradford-on-Avon

Horningsham

102

98 The Bunch of Grapes

Ancient pub with modern ethos

A family-run pub in a rural town may be an unlikely setting for new-wave gastronomy, but it's where talented chef Tony Casey plays with flavour, texture and style to create dishes that dazzle. He and his wife, Maylee Speller, took over The Bunch of Grapes in Bradford-on-Avon in 2018 and have since achieved a *Michelin* recommendation, *The Good Food Guide* entry and two AA rosettes.

Kickstart your visit with cocktails while you ponder whether to plump for à la carte or push the boat out with a five- or seven-course tasting menu. Either way, quality seasonal ingredients take centre stage in dishes such as pork belly and shoulder with turnip cake, spring roll, pak choi, purple sprouting and hoisin.

For those seeking something more casual, the bar menu offers the likes of salt and pepper squid with garlic mayo, chilli, lime and spring onion alongside pub classics. Whatever you order, keep your phone nearby to snap a photo before you dig in – Tony's plating is eminently Instagrammable.

The interior styling is equally easy on the eye. An imposing bar with an impressive collection of spirits and glassware provides the central focal point while, on the first floor, striking blue walls and eye-catching artwork provide a visual feast to complement Tony's dishes.

Trencherman's tip

Swing by sister venue The Bunch of Bakes next door. This new addition to the business is the place to pick up handmade baked goods including flaky croissants and artisan bread.

Chef Tony Casey | **3-course dinner from** £32.50 | **Seats** 60

thebunchofgrapes.com | 14 Silver Street, Bradford-on-Avon, Wiltshire, BA15 1JY | 01225 863650

99 Lucknam Park Hotel & Spa

Austen-esque escapism

Lazing beneath a parasol on the lawn of this Palladian mansion near Bath, while sipping a Lucknam French Martini and gazing over a landscape straight out of an Austen novel, is a truly special experience.

From the moment guests arrive (and make their way along a mile-long driveway that clips the 500 acres of manicured grounds), they're enchanted by their beguiling surroundings. Yet, while the setting is alluring, it's the food that's secured Lucknam's reputation as one of the UK's best country house hotels.

Restaurant Hywel Jones is the Michelin-adorned star around which the Lucknam Park experience orbits. Executive chef Hywel's 18-year streak in the prestigious guide has made his eponymous restaurant a bucket-list destination for discerning foodies.

Discover the chef's prowess in seasonal and signature tasting menus, and plump for the wine pairings to elevate the experience to euphoric heights.

For a casual lunch or laid-back supper, the contemporary Brasserie offers wood-fired delights like gilt-head bream with roasted garlic prawns, broad bean and wild garlic linguini with verjus butter. When the weather's good, huge bi-fold doors open to create an alfresco dining vibe befitting the garden setting.

Trencherman's tip

Make the most of the hotel's profusion of facilities – including a spa, gym and cookery school – and activities such as horse riding, cycling, tennis, clay pigeon shooting and croquet.

Chef Hywel Jones | **3-course dinner from** £55 (at Brasserie) | **Seats** 56, plus 48 in Brasserie
Bedrooms 42, plus 7 cottages | **Room rate from** £310 | **EV charging**
luacknampark.co.uk | Colerne, Wiltshire, SN14 8AZ | 01225 742777

Best Trencherman's Pub

The Castle Inn

'To win this during our first year of being in Trencherman's is a great achievement'

Jamie Barnett, head chef

Left to right: Ieuan Davies and Jamie Barnett of The Castle Inn
with Ruud Jansen Venneboer of South West 660 (event partner)

100 The Castle Inn

Exceptional experience with local charm

The Cotswolds village of Castle Combe, with its honey-coloured cottages and picture-postcard setting, has often been hailed as the prettiest village in England, but its most delightful asset is undoubtedly The Castle Inn.

The 12th-century inn treats diners to a thoughtfully curated menu of seasonally inspired dishes. The team pride themselves on sourcing the finest regional ingredients, which they use to craft dishes as classic as the surroundings. It's a formula that's working: the inn was crowned Best Trencherman's Pub in 2023 and has picked up a *Michelin* listing.

The knock-out Sunday lunches deserve a special mention. Incredible cuts are sourced from Origin Meats near Bristol, with the slow-cooked Frampton on Severn lamb shoulder for two being particularly noteworthy. Arrive early, though, as it sells out most weeks.

Not a meat eater? The Castle Inn's satay of Bromham cauliflower with chilli pak choi, cucumber, toasted peanuts and coriander won't disappoint.

Drinks are sourced with as much care as the food, and a recent addition to the bar is fellow B Corp business Toast. The brewery crafts ale from surplus bread to reduce food waste and donates all its profits to a charity with the same aim.

Trencherman's tip

Make a night of it and stay in one of 12 immaculately furnished rooms.

Chef Jamie Barnett | **3-course dinner from** £35 | **Seats** 40
Bedrooms 12 | **Room rate from** £155 | **EV charging**

thecastleinn.co.uk | West Street, Castle Combe, Chippenham, Wiltshire, SN14 7HN | 01249 783030

Magazines build relationships

We create award-winning titles; talk to us about making your in-house magazine

saltmedia.co.uk

101 The Manor House

Star-quality elegance

Nestled in the picturesque Cotswolds village of Castle Combe, The Manor House exudes a magnetic energy that begins on the winding drive leading up to the 14th-century retreat.

With a Michelin-starred restaurant, alfresco dining, The Full Glass Bar (180 gins and counting), lounges for coffee or afternoon tea, private dining rooms and even a country pub (The Castle Inn), there's a dining experience for every occasion.

Taking its name from the river that runs through the hotel grounds, the Bybrook restaurant is the jewel in the crown. Executive chef Rob Potter has retained a Michelin star here since 2017. He leads a brigade of talented chefs in creating seasonal dishes that utilise local and British ingredients, enhanced by expertly matched fine wines.

Feast on Cornish wild turbot with white asparagus, Petrossian caviar and seaweed butter; Herdwick lamb with morel, wild garlic and kohlrabi; or Yorkshire wagyu with yukon gold potato and celeriac.

Make it an occasion by staying over in the historic hotel or mews cottages and exploring the Italian gardens, Bybrook River and 365 acres of grounds that include an 18-hole championship golf course. You can even bring the chopper – The Manor House has its own helipad.

Trencherman's tip

Feeling romantic? The Bybrook dine-and-stay package includes a tasting menu for two, a luxurious night in a room of your choice and breakfast the next morning.

Chef Robert Potter | **7-course tasting menu** £145 | **Seats** 75
Bedrooms 50 | **Room rate from** £290 | **EV charging**

exclusive.co.uk/the-manor-house | Castle Combe, Chippenham, Wiltshire, SN14 7HX | 01249 782206

102 The Bath Arms at Longleat

Seasonal dining at the heart of the British countryside

Established in 1736, The Bath Arms is a traditional yet stylish country inn on the edge of the unspoiled Longleat Estate in Wiltshire.

The relaxed, dog-friendly venue is just two hours from London and 30 minutes from Bath, and is a charming environment in which to linger over a long lunch or sumptuous supper. Chef Jack Chapman and his talented team are committed to utilising the abundant seasonal Wiltshire produce on their doorstep. Meat and game are sourced from local farms and the Longleat Estate itself, while the fish is landed daily on the south coast.

The menu is carefully designed to reflect each season: sample venison haunch with heritage beetroot, celeriac puree, bolognese, feuille de brick tart, juniper jus and chocolate, followed by Beckford affogato with salted caramel ice cream, espresso and rum.

The bar is stocked with traditional ales (many locally brewed, including the inn's own Horning Ale), world-class wines from sister venue The Beckford Bottle Shop in Bath and classic cocktails. Delicious snacks are available throughout the day. In summer, dining spills out onto the sunny terrace and into the lush gardens.

Trencherman's tip

This is an ideal base from which to explore Longleat's landscaped gardens, Elizabethan architecture and famous safari park. Stay in one of 16 chic bedrooms, complete with crisp sheets, beautiful views and Bramley products made just down the road by The Beckford Group.

Chef Jack Chapman | **3-course dinner from** £40 | **Seats** 58 | **Bedrooms** 16 | **Room rate from** £130

batharmsinn.com | Horningsham, Warminster, Wiltshire, BA12 7LY | 01985 844308

103 Sign of the Angel

Romantic inn steeped in history

Visitors flock to the National Trust village of Lacock for its cobbled streets and stone cottages, which have graced the screens of many a costume drama – including *Downton Abbey* and *Pride and Prejudice*.

In-the-know gastronomes make a beeline for Sign of the Angel, a 15th-century coaching inn that oozes olde-worlde charm while serving up modern British cooking.

Head chef Dan Mack seeks out sustainable produce from farmers, growers and butchers, which he uses to craft dishes such as pan-seared Cornish scallops with a spicy crab bisque, and herb-crusted lamb rump with carrot puree, spring greens, and lamb and rosemary croquettes.

Stop by during the day to take advantage of Dan's excellent dishes with a tempting lunch offer of three courses for £35. Or make a night of it and book one of the five homely rooms – each with original period features – for a quintessentially English country inn experience.

Trencherman's tip

The relaxing pub is a charmingly romantic spot all year round. In summer, while away the hours in the sun-trap garden devouring small plates or a cream tea. Winter provides the opportunity to cosy up by the open fire and dine by candlelight.

Chef Dan Mack | **3-course dinner from** £40 | **Seats** 50 | **Bedrooms** 5 | **Room rate from** £120

signoftheangel.co.uk | 6 Church Street, Lacock, Chippenham, Wiltshire, SN15 2LB | 01249 730230

Gloucestershire & Oxfordshire

Restaurants listed in the guide correspond to the numbers plotted on the map.

All locations are approximate

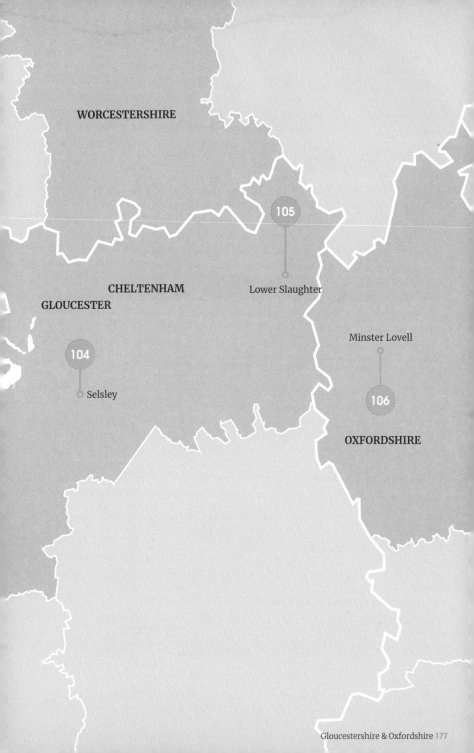

WORCESTERSHIRE

105

CHELTENHAM

Lower Slaughter

GLOUCESTER

Minster Lovell

104

106

Selsley

OXFORDSHIRE

104 The Bell Inn

Award-winning Cotswold dining pub

Traditional country inns may be ten-a-penny in the Cotswolds, but it's rare to find one that, like The Bell Inn, is a proper dog-friendly local that also serves award-winning gourmet food.

You're as welcome to walk in wearing wellies and enjoy a pint and a pickled egg with a four-legged friend in tow as you are to dress up and indulge in a three-course feast from a menu that exhibits the best of British produce.

Chef-owner Mark Payne is big on seasonal and local ingredients, including lamb from the neighbouring fields and veg from his own allotment and kitchen garden. The line-up is refreshingly simple, with an emphasis on quality ingredients cooked well. A braised blade of beef with girolles falls apart to the touch, while the gluten-free batter on the fish and chips is fried to crisp perfection.

Make sure you're sporting an elasticated waistband to take full advantage of desserts like pistachio crème brûlée, and apricot and frangipane tatin with crème fraîche sorbet. Or, for a lighter pud, try the 'gin'gato – a scoop of homemade vanilla ice cream drenched, affogato-style, in rhubarb and ginger gin liqueur.

Trencherman's tip

The inn houses 75 artisan gins – many made locally – so book a room for the night and sample a few.

Chef Mark Payne | **3-course dinner from** £32 | **Seats** 58 | **Bedrooms** 3 | **Room rate from** £90

thebellinnselsley.com | Bell Lane, Selsley, Gloucestershire, GL5 5JY | 01453 753801

105 The Slaughters Manor House

Contemporary luxury in the Cotswolds

Starched white table linen, pastel-hued furnishings and floor-to-ceiling windows create an elegant setting in which to dine at The Slaughters Manor House.

This beautiful 17th-century manor in the Cotswolds is steeped in history yet exudes contemporary luxury and comfort. And nowhere is this more prevalent than in head chef Nik Chappell's artful creations, which reflect the refined mood.

For a light and zingy dish, Cornish crab quiche with lemon mayo and chamomile hits the spot, while heartier appetites will appreciate the indulgence of loin of Cotswold venison with red cabbage, blackberries and sauce grand veneur, or veal ribeye with tongue, cheek, onion and truffle.

Pre-dinner drinks can be enjoyed in the ritzy cocktail lounge, which has a 360-degree bar where visitors can perch on blush-pink stools while their server rustles up cocktails or pours spirits from an extensive drinks list.

For the full Slaughters' experience, book one of the characterful guestrooms. Each is named and styled after members of the Whitmore family, who owned the manor for many generations.

Trencherman's tip

If visiting for afternoon tea, be sure to take a turn around the beautifully manicured lawns and garden.

Chef Nik Chappell | **3-course dinner from** £85 | **Seats** 45 | **Bedrooms** 19 | **Room rate from** £285
slaughtersmanor.co.uk | Copsehill Road, Lower Slaughter, Gloucestershire, GL54 2HP | 01451 820456

106 Minster Mill

Glamorous retreat for gourmets

You needn't travel far from the dreaming spires of Oxford to experience the uncompromising luxury of Cotswolds retreat Minster Mill, part of the Andrew Brownsword Hotels collection.

Set in glorious grounds, the honey-coloured converted mill is a rural idyll in the village of Minster Lovell. Charming Cotswold stone buildings and barns are flanked by 65 acres of riverside gardens.

Kick off a visit in style with a classic cocktail in the lofty gallery bar or head to the garden terrace to sip while surrounded by wildflower meadows, woodland and the burble of the River Windrush.

Dinner is served beneath the vaulted ceilings and oak beams of the three-AA-rosette restaurant, where new head chef Andrew Campbell specialises in contemporary British

cooking. Creative flair and a commitment to supporting regional producers sees each artfully devised dish fused with a local twist. Wine and Champagne from the extensive Brownsword cellar complete the experience.

At other times of day, the hotel is a picturesque destination at which to enjoy lunch or a Laurent-Perrier Champagne afternoon tea. Add sleek Scandi-style bedrooms, a garden spa and traditional amusements including croquet and tennis, and there are plentiful enticements to extend a stay.

Trencherman's tip

Pop across the road to sister property Old Swan for the more casual pleasures of a hand-raised pie and glass of cool ale in a traditional pub setting.

Chef Andrew Campbell | **3-course dinner from** £70 | **Seats** 45
Bedrooms 38 | **Room rate from** £225

minstermill.co.uk | Minster Lovell, Oxfordshire, OX29 0RN | 01993 774441

Index

Index

Index

PHOTOGRAPHY

Tom Asteriades
Matt Austin
Tim J Baker
J-Ph Baudey
Mark Bolton
Kieran Brimson

Adj Brown
Josh Campbell
Mark Cleghorn
Drew Gibson
Exposure Photo Agency
A Gilbert
Sam Harris

Guy Harrop
Matthew Hawkey
John Hersey
Nick Hook
Elizabeth Melvin
Lee Searle
Nick Smith

Pink Wave Photography
Polly Stock
Stephen Studd
Angela Ward Brown
Elliott White
Marc Wilson
Arabelle Zhuang Yuru

Notes

For details of special dishes and drinks you've experienced at Trencherman's restaurants

Notes

For details of special dishes and drinks you've experienced at Trencherman's restaurants

Notes

For details of special dishes and drinks you've
experienced at Trencherman's restaurants